18.00

It's Better to Be Lucky Than Good

It's Better to Be Lucky Than Good

an autobiography of a real cowboy

Merle Aus

Book and Cover designed by Kristin K. Aus.

Edited by Rose Marie Aus, Kristin Aus
and Bruce Bainbridge.

Copyright © 2006 by Seven Mile Publishing
454 Road 544
Glendive, Montana 59330

ISBN 0-615-13097-6
First edition.

Printed in U. S. A.

To My Wife, Rose Marie

> *Because June 9, 1960 was the very luckiest day of my life.*

Acknowledgements

A big thank you to Rose Marie, Kristin and Bruce for reading the manuscript and making the necessary corrections. Rose Marie's expertise was invaluable and she spent untold hours proofreading. A special thank you to Kristin, our resident computer expert, for helping me learn what computer skills I could absorb and then doing the rest herself. Without her knowledge and expertise this book could not have been completed.

A very special thank you to Valerie Hemingway for reading the manuscript and for some very useful comments and suggestions.

Thank you also to Rosanne Bos for typing the original manuscript and to my niece, Lisa Wutzke Bleth for helping to find a printer.

Thank you to Wilmer and Grace, Shirla and another niece Yvonne Deitz for lending me some pictures.

And a special thank you to all the good people who have made my life enjoyable, which is just about everyone I have known.

Table of Contents

List of Illustrations

It's Better to Be Lucky Than Good

It is so full of minute detail of a period that is now past. I think it is valuable as a slice of local history. It is rare to find an amateur memoir which has such careful recollections and documentations.

Valerie Hemingway
Author of *Running with the Bulls*
My Years with the Hemingways

Prologue

Will Rogers, the famous humorist, once said, it's better to be lucky than good. I am probably not good at anything in particular but I've been lucky at times.

This book is mostly about me and it's all the truth. I have no writing experience nor do I have a broad vocabulary. So why am I writing a book? Well, it's something I've never done before and I like a challenge. This is not about a celebrity but about a common ordinary person who has lived a long time. Perhaps my generation has seen more changes, both good and bad, than any other generation in history. The computer is hard for some of us old timers to comprehend but it is one of the modern inventions that will do such amazing things it's unbelievable. That is one of the good changes and it certainly has been a handy tool in writing this book.

I wrote most of this in longhand and then had a retired language teacher do most of the typing. I told her to type it as it was written because I thought my grammar was pretty good. But I'm finding out that is not so. I had to get Kristin to transfer it all unto Rose Marie's computer. It underlines in red all my mistakes. So I'm learning to type again. I'm getting faster. I can now type with both hands, (one finger of each.)

I am fortunate to have had good hard-working Christian parents who raised 7 children, who got along well and had a lot of friends. My parents had both good and bad luck, and like most early day homesteaders, didn't accumulate a lot of wealth, but managed to make it through the great depression and lived a long life. A few days before he died Dad told me he had paid all his debts. Not every one could say that in those days.

The luckiest and happiest time of my life was the summer of 1959. While doing a bit of acting in a play called Old Four Eyes, I met the most wonderful girl I had ever met.

Rose Marie Goetz had come to work in the show too, and it didn't take us long to decide we wanted to spend the rest of our lives together. We were married the following spring. It's the smartest thing I have ever done in my life and it's been wonderful. We have been best friends ever since.

Kristin was born in 1965, making me a proud papa. She took to horses at a young age and she was very successful in horse shows. She also took to books at an early age. If she wasn't out with the horses she was probably in her room with a book. We were glad she liked to read. She graduated from Carroll College at the head of her class and became a C.P.A. and then went on to get a Master's Degree in agriculture at C.S.U.

Kristin met Bruce Bainbridge at C. S. U. They were married and moved to Montana where they are both teaching at Dawson College. They also have some Paint horses and they do the heavy work here at the ranch. With them nearby we will hopefully be able to stay here for a few more years. Bruce has a Ph.D. in Ag. Economics. People tell us both he and Kristin are great teachers. Bruce also has other talents. He can and does do anything that needs to be done on the ranch, from building fence, to putting in water lines, doing electrical work or welding. He does all the things I wish I could still do and he moves faster then anyone I know. He has a way of getting horses gentle and I like the way he works with colts to get them to load in a horse trailer without getting them excited or nervous. When Rose Marie and I have company for dinner and need help in the kitchen, Bruce is good help there too. He and Kristin are both very considerate and they take good care of us in our old age.

Ranching has always been my primary occupation but I've done other things part time. I bought a truck (with borrowed money) when I was 19 years old and eventually ran 2 trucks. I sold out after 6 years.

I have also done other things like saddle making, sheep shearing, rodeoing, acting, real estate sales, bought and sold ranches, broke a few horses, and have done some wood work and carpentry. I also taught saddle making at Dawson Community College for 15 years. Everything I've

Bruce Bainbridge and Kristin Aus

done I've enjoyed so I'll say I have been lucky if not always so good.

I hope you enjoy reading my simple effort at writing a book. If you do, tell others. If you don't, don't bother to mention it.

Chapter 1

Homesteading

A four year old boy was missing. He had been playing outside on a nice sunny day in early spring and now in spite of frantic calls from his mother and two older sisters he was nowhere to be seen. The ranch was built beside a creek. It was running high from the recent snow melt and the mother was afraid the boy had fallen into the water and was swept away. The sisters were supposed to be watching after the boy but each thought the other was doing it. And he just slipped away.

But the boy was in no trouble – yet. He was just playing hide and seek with the ones who were looking for him. When he heard them call the first time he was behind a little A shaped coop that was used to set turkey hens or chicken hens when they were setting on eggs to hatch. He slipped inside the empty coop and thought they will never find him there.

He was right. They didn't think to look in the coop for him and he soon tired of the game. Like most kids his age his attention span was short. He finally came out of his hiding place and began walking toward the house feeling pretty proud that he had found such a good hiding place. The mother was a very gentle loving person but when she saw the boy she lost her temper and became angry. That was as close as I ever came to getting a spanking.

That little boy was me and I got a lecture I never forgot. That was the first event of my life that I can remember. Even though it was nearly 77 years ago it is still as clear as if it had happened last week.

This took place in southwestern North Dakota. Scranton was our nearest town and that is where I was born. I am the youngest of nine children. Seven of us grew up to be adults. I had one brother and five sisters to wait on me so I became pretty spoiled but I liked it.

The folks were one of the very earliest homesteaders in that part of the country. It was 1905 when they built their homestead shack and 1906 when the family came out. The claim was 60 miles southwest of Dickinson. That was the closest town then and that was where they unloaded their immigrant car. Their homestead claim was the south east ¼ of section 14 township 132 range 99 Bowman county North Dakota but later they moved to the north west ¼ of section 24. I heard Dad say when they got off the train with Mother and a baby girl about one year old and their worldly possessions, all the money he had was a $5 gold piece. He had four horses, a wagon and one cow. He started to haul freight then with his four horse team. The country was filling up with settlers and freighting was good for several years. Since it was 60 miles one way to the railroad it took several days to make the trip. Mother would worry in the winter when a blizzard came up and Dad was out hauling. Several times he had to stop in the night, because he couldn't see the trail, and walk around the wagon all night to keep from freezing to death. Mother would keep a kerosene lamp burning in the windows all night in case Dad was close to making it home. On one trip he had a passenger who wanted to go to sleep. Dad knew that if he did go to sleep he would freeze to death, so he used his horse whip to keep him walking and they both survived.

Those must have been tough times especially for women. With no electricity or plumbing they had to carry water in and then carry it out again. They raised big families and big gardens if it rained. They seldom got to town and neighbors were few and far between, especially in the early years. Mother used to say how lonesome she had been before they finally got some neighbors. The area where they settled had very few trees, just choke cherries or June berries and a few willows along the creeks. Mother talked about how she missed being where there were trees. They came from Southeastern South Dakota where trees grew everywhere. On the other hand Dad was probably pretty satisfied. The country was still open even after some settlers moved in. Stock could be turned loose in the fall and there was free grazing until spring. I can remember as a kid each spring the neighbors would round up all the horses that had wintered out and each one would trail his stock to his own place. They usually corralled them at our place to sort them. That was pretty exciting for me to watch all those men working on horseback.

My brother Wilmer was almost ten years older than I and I idolized him so much that I wanted to follow him wherever he went. I'm sure I was a big nuisance but he was very patient with me. Some times he let me ride with him and I'd feel pretty important but if he had to go very far or very fast I had to stay at home. I remember one day he said I could go with him. He was riding a young horse he was breaking and I was on old Peanuts. He was the only horse Dad had at the time that was gentle enough for me. I was five at the time. Old Peanuts was pretty lazy and I wasn't keeping up very good so Wilmer cut a willow branch for me to use for a quirt so he wouldn't have to wait for me. Well, Peanuts objected to that and when I woke up I was in the house on a bed. Old Peanuts had bucked me off. Wilmer said I went over the horses' head, turned a summersault and came down flat on my back. That was the first time that happened and the last was 60 years later and there were also several times in between.

Chapter 2

My First Horse

The summer I was seven, Dad gave me a two year old sorrel filly. She had never been touched, of course, and was running out with a bunch of other mostly wild horses.

I immediately started to bug Wilmer to catch her and break her for me. One day he and a neighbor friend, Bud Sipma, about the same age, had some horses in the corral and my filly was with them. I must have begged Wilmer to catch her until finally he said, "Well, go ahead and catch her then." I'm sure he didn't think I could rope her but on the second try I caught her. I think I surprised everyone including myself. In those days we didn't know any way to get a halter on a wild horse other than to rope it and dally to a snubbing post. With the filly caught, Wilmer didn't have any choice but to halter break it and not long afterwards he was riding her. Two year olds weren't usually ridden back then but this was an exception. Colts weren't fed as much as they are nowadays so they weren't developed until they were three or four years old. When she was broke gentle enough for me to ride, I pretty much lived on her every summer until school started in the fall. Besides that she raised me a colt just about every year. If I was herding sheep or chasing cattle the colt would tag along. Dad suggested I call the filly Flossie so that was her name.

Billy Carter was a horse buyer from Scranton, North Dakota, and he came out to buy a load of horses from Dad. He sure wanted to buy my horse too but I wouldn't let her go. I was awfully proud to have my own horse. I kept her all of her useful life. We used horses so much back then. It wasn't just for pleasure but it was our transportation. We didn't have four wheel drive pickups then.

Dad had some good horses. One he called Socks was well respected in the community around Scranton. He was jet black with a bald face and four white stockings. He was so high lifed and eager to go that I wasn't allowed to ride him until both of us were older. There were many stories told of the extra-ordinary endurance the horse had. It sounded as if Dad would do more than his share on a long trail behind a herd of cattle or horses and Socks would still seem to be eager to go and the other riders' horses would be played out.

One day after Socks and I were both a little older, Dad was gone and I saddled Socks. When dad got home I was riding his horse. He didn't say anything so from then on I rode him regularly. I did the same thing with a team I wasn't supposed to be able to handle. There was another team that was older and gentler which I was supposed to use. One day when Dad came home from town I had the young team hitched to a slip scraper and I was cleaning a corral. A slip scraper has two handles to use to fill it or to dump the load so there are no hands free to handle the lines. So it is best to have a well broke team because the lines are tied together and put around the driver's neck and under one arm. When Dad got home he saw I was getting along ok. He didn't say anything to me and I didn't say anything to him. I used that team from then on if he wasn't using them.

Chapter 3

Hard Times

Dad bought a new car, a 1925 Chevy. I was told he traded a railroad carload of horses for the car. That was probably about 25 head. Dad, of course, had never driven a car before. The first time he took the family to church he forgot how to stop it so he circled the church saying "Whoa." He finally got it figured out but driving didn't come naturally for him though he drove until he was in his 80's and I never knew him to have an accident. During the '30's the car broke down and dad traded it to a neighbor, Art Norby, for a straw pile to feed the stock. We didn't have a car then for a few years.

The next car we had was a 1930 Durrant. That was a pretty fancy car in its day with four doors and six cylinders. Then a few years later we got a Hudson-Terraplane. After that we drove Chevys and Fords like everyone else.

My folks had built up a fair sized herd of cattle in the 1920's. But when the hard times hit, the Bank of Scranton decided it wanted them so they sent some

Left to Right:
Wilmer on the new Chevy, Dad is holding me, Fern,
Mother, June, Thelma, Shirla and Uncle Ben Aus.

cowboys out to gather them and trail them to the rail-road. Foreclosure was common those days. The folks also had some sheep that were not mortgaged and that is what helped us survive the depression. It was a hard life but everyone was hard up those days.

The banker in Scranton then was named Christopher. His son was Warren Christopher the government diplomat under President Jimmie Carter. Small town boy makes good.

There was no money but it didn't cost much to live either. There was no electricity bill, no cable or inter-net, taxes were low, and no one carried insurance. A five gallon can of kerosene kept the lamps burning for a long time. In the summer we went to bed when it got dark because the moths would fly down the lamp chimney and break the mantle. We had no refrigera-tion but a root cellar kept the milk and butter cool. Also the homemade root beer was kept there.

Needless to say we didn't go out to dinner. (It was called supper. Dinner was at noon and lunch was coffee in the afternoon.) Our main type of social event was to go to the neighbors to visit. The older folks would visit or play cards and us kids would play ball or some other games or go swimming in some muddy pond of water if it wasn't all dried up.

We used the car only to go to town or to church or when the whole family was going somewhere. If we kids were going somewhere we went horseback. I remember one night Wilmer and I rode over to visit our good friends the Sipmas. They were a big family and we spent a lot of time together. This was a warm summer night and we stayed later than usual and it started to rain. Sipmas invited us to stay until morn-ing but Wilmer thought we should go home. I thought anything Wilmer said was alright so we started home.

It was four miles home and the rain poured down all the way.

There was a lot of lightning and thunder and the electricity would spark on the tips of the horses' ears. That was pretty spooky for a six year old kid but as long as I was with my big brother I thought I was safe.

In the winter there would be card parties around the neighborhood. Some folks would come in cars but there was always the problem of radiators freezing up. The water had to be drained and then filled up again when it was time to go home. Anti freeze was invented a few years later so that made things more convenient. Some came with a team and a sleigh. The kids would be riding down in the box with plenty of straw and robes to keep them warm. Some nights it would be pitch dark but if the teams got headed in the right direction they would find the way home.

We used to think it was fun to go berry picking in the summer. Around the 4th of July the June berries would be ripe. Dad would hook a team to the buggy and mother would pack a picnic lunch and we'd go up the creek looking for berries. A dish of ripe June berries with thick fresh cream and sugar was a real treat. You can't buy thick cream like we had then.

During the depression of the early 1930's, money was scarce. I didn't know what an allowance for kids was. But then I didn't need money because I didn't get to town anyway. One year there were two bum lambs. Dad told my sister Shirla and me if we took care of them we could have them. We were pretty excited about that and the lambs grew up to be ewes and we got the money for the wool and lambs that they produced each year. That was our allowance for the year.

I was probably about 10 years old. We were still living near Scranton, jack rabbits were pretty thick and fur buyers were paying 10 cents apiece for them. All I had was a BB gun, but Wilmer had a single shot 22 and he was away at CCC camp. I was allowed to take the rifle out to shoot rabbits. Or I should say shoot at rabbits. I wasn't a very good shot at that age but I must have gotten a few. At least I didn't give up.

The junk dealers also bought bones. There were a lot of old bleached out bones on the prairie those days, an accumulation of many, many years. It had only been 60 or so years since the last buffalo were killed so I think a lot of the bones were buffalo. I probably didn't know the difference between a buffalo skull and a cow skull. Buffalo skulls were so common nobody bothered to save one for a souvenir. I remember seeing the remains of buffalo wallows on the prairie. The buffalo created wallows by continuing to paw the ground in a small area until they would have a hollowed out depression in the ground where they could lie down and roll in the loose dirt so the flies didn't bother them quite so much.

I wasn't old enough to be trusted with a team and wagon, but I had a little wagon I pulled behind a saddle horse so I set out to gather bones. My plan was to haul them home and pile them up and then have Dad haul them to town with his team and wagon. I don't remember anyone in the neighborhood who had a pickup then. This was in the depression of the 1930s.

It was slow going, but I had lots of time and it gave me an excuse to ride a horse. I worked at this all one summer and had a pretty good pile of bones. Then one day everyone left and when we got home, my pile of bones was all gone. Someone had been watching me and waited for the opportunity to make an easy buck stealing from a kid. He probably needed the money, too. Everyone did those days.

There wasn't much to do to keep busy when I was a kid. I spent a lot of time horseback pretending I was looking after the cattle but actually I was just killing time. I liked to ride a little fast. Wilmer had a few accidents with horses and he tried to impress on me that a horse might step in a hole and fall, so I shouldn't run a horse unless there was a good reason. So I would ride at a walk until I got out of sight of the house and then I'd whip and spur.

When I got a little older, Dad asked me if I'd take the sheep out and herd them as their pasture was getting short. I felt sorry for myself because sheep move so slow, and it was boring out there by myself, but I did it until school started.

I didn't mind school. There were quite a few boys in our country school so there were games to play at recess time. When I was in the first grade, my sister Fern was in the eighth grade and Shirla was a 3rd grader. We had 3 miles to go so we had to start out pretty early. When I was in the 7th and 8th grade, I would go to school early and start a fire in the furnace before the teacher got there. I don't think that hurt my grades any.

Chapter 4

Our Family

Iknew only one of my grandparents. My paternal grandmother was living in Sioux Falls, South Dakota, in 1938 when I started going to high school near there in Canton, South Dakota. She lived to be 93. I only saw her a few times. My paternal grandfather was a carpenter in Norway and came to the States on a sailing ship. They sailed up the St. Lawrence River and then went to Canton where he built houses. Some of the houses are still standing. It must have been hard work building houses those days without any power tools and I understand some were built with wooden pegs instead of nails. He also built furniture. Some of the pieces I've seen are very ornate and are still being used.

My maternal grandparents also came from Norway. They settled at Canton too. They were beekeepers and produced honey for a living. Two of their sons followed in the bee business and every fall Uncle Louie would bring us a five gallon can of honey so us kids

Mother and Dad's wedding picture, 1904.

would have peanut butter and honey sandwiches in our school lunches.

My parents were married in Canton and farmed there one year before homesteading in Southwestern North Dakota.

My oldest sister Blanche was married before I was born so I didn't see her much that I remember. Esther was next oldest. She was a nurse and later became a Deaconess at a Lutheran hospital in a suburb of Chicago. She would come home for a vacation most every summer.

Thelma was an elementary school teacher and later married Lloyd Deitz. They ran a store at Gorham, North Dakota. During the depression they left for Coeur d'Alene, Idaho, where they had a photography studio.

Wilmer was the fourth born. He was in the army during WWII. When he came back, he and I ranched together. After 9 years he bought my interest in the

Wilmer and Grace

ranch and has been there ever since. He married Grace Homelvig. Their son Gordon is operating the ranch now. This is west of Amidon on the edge of the Little Missouri Badlands.

Sister Fern came next. She married Al Wutzke, a career army officer. They lived wherever the military sent them. When he retired as a major, they settled in Coeur d'Alene, Idaho. Fern had a twin brother, but he died at birth.

June was next, but she died of diphtheria at age 9.

Shirla is the youngest sister. She taught in a rural school where she met and married Howard Olson. They farmed near Scranton, North Dakota, and for a time near Long Prairie, Minnesota.

Then I came along and there were no more babies.

Blanche and her husband Kenneth Smith had three children, Kenneth Jr, Howard Dean and Viva Ann. Thelma and Lloyd had two,Yvonne and Wesley. Esther never married. Wilmer and Grace have four, Gary, Susan, Sharon, and Gordon. Fern and Al had four, Ronald, Gary, Warren, and Carroll. Shirla and Howard had Betty, David, Larry, Mark, and Nancy, five in all. Rose Marie and I have Kristin. Shirla's family tree is by far the biggest. As I write this, she has 22 grandchildren and 23 great-grandchildren.

Mother was a small woman. She probably stood about five feet tall. She was a real lady, kind and gentle, but one who could be tough if she needed to be. To raise seven children under homestead conditions with absolutely no modern conveniences she had to be tough. One good thing there was a 20 year spread between Blanche, the oldest and me, the youngest, so the older could help with the younger.

Mother not only was a good cook and homemaker she was very talented with her old treadle Singer sewing machine and her fancy needle work. She won blue ribbons whenever I could talk her into showing her work at the county fair. She also helped with the chores. She would saddle a horse or harness a team if it needed to be done. She always had a big garden and got a lot of pleasure with her flowers.

I think I was about six years old when one day I was going to ride out to bring in the milk cows. (That was my job.) Dad had traded for a saddle horse that was supposed to be gentle enough for anyone. It was a good looking grey horse and dad had left it saddled and tied up for me. When I started to go in the stall with a bridle in my hand, the horse moved over to pin me against the wall. I tried it a couple times and then went to the house for help. He tried the same thing with mother but she hit him on the butt with the bridle and spoke sharply to the horse and I never had any trouble after that. A little discipline works on horses too.

Not many years after that Mother became ill and could no longer do any heavy work. The doctors

Dad and Mother at their 50th wedding anniversary in 1954.

couldn't seem to find the problem and for the rest of her life she had to take it easy. She could still do her fancy needle work and she liked to read. Her mind was still sharp when she died at age 91.

Dad was 6 foot 1 and weighed over 200 pounds. He was always healthy and stood straight. He was still riding horseback when he was 80 years old and he always sat in the front row at the livestock sales ring in Bowman every Monday.

Then one day when he was 84 years old he got sick. The doctor didn't know why. He hated being in the hospital. He said it was a disgrace for him to be there. He passed away peacefully a few weeks later.

Wilmer, Shirla and I are the only ones in the family still living, but all of the siblings except June lived well beyond the average life expectancy.

At one time we were separated around the country and the seven of us lived in seven different states. Maybe that is one reason we all got along so well.

Shirla is only a couple years older than I so we spent a lot of time together when we were little. Before I was old enough to ride a horse by myself, my favorite pastime was to play with a stick horse. Shirla would rather cut out paper dolls from an old catalog. So we would make a deal. If she would play stick horse with me I would play paper dolls with her. Since I was the youngest and the most spoiled we would always play stick horse first. Then I would hope mother would call us in for supper or to do some errand or anything so I could renege on my promise to play paper dolls with my sister.

Mother saw to it we had a Christian upbringing. Dad didn't talk a lot but taught by example. He was very well respected wherever he went. Going to church was an important part of our lives although in the early years it was often hard to get there. The community didn't have a real church building for Lutherans but met a couple times a month in the Woodberry School building about 10 miles from our home. A minister from Reeder would come out and preach. Now and then he would preach in Norwegian. That was pretty boring for the young folks who couldn't understand the language, but they were expected to sit quietly. The congregation eventually built a church. It was called Cedar Lutheran Church.

I was probably the most rambunctious of the family. I liked a little adventure. A short memory is not necessarily a bad thing at times. I've mellowed some these later years.

You cannot choose your relatives. That is a fact, but if I could I wouldn't make a single change. Our family has been very compatible. The same goes for my in-laws. The folks that say they can't get along

Mother and her kids at her 80th birthday party in 1965
Back row: Esther, Thelma, Fern, Shirla, Blanche
Seated: Wilmer, Mother, Me

with their mother-in-law haven't been as lucky as I was. Freda was a wonderful person who was always thinking of other people. Everyone who came to her door was offered something to eat. She worked hard all of her life and gave generously to many charities. She lived to the ripe old age of 97. Unfortunately, Rose Marie's father passed away when she was only five years old so I didn't get to know him. The sisters in law were all a chip off the old block, generous and hard working and fun to be around.

We often spent holidays at Freda's home in Harvey, North Dakota. Freda was a great cook and of course everyone that came would bring good things to eat. After the meal there would be card playing because Freda liked to play cards and was very good at it. I would feel sorry for whoever got me for a partner because I didn't get much practice at cards. I had to depend on luck. But it was all just for fun. At the gathering would be the three sisters in law, Helen and Gunnar Davidson and their five children, Marian and John Maguire and six children, Jo Ann and Steve and their two and us with Kristin. It was a big gathering and it was fun. I believe I have been accepted into the family and they all supported me when I was sick.

Going back again to the drought and depression and hard times of the 1930's -- Many people left the country. Our rural school went from 20 kids down to nine in just a couple years. I believe more families would have left, but just didn't have the money to travel anywhere. I remember the folks talking about the lack of money. It must have been a stressful time for all parents in the community, especially for those with big families. The depression made a lasting impression on me. I still think of the hardships we went through, but we survived and compared to people that live through hurricanes and earthquakes I guess we were lucky.

Our folks were determined that my sisters graduate from high school. They had to live away from home and work for their room and board. The same was true for college.

Chapter 5

Grasshoppers

President Franklin D. Roosevelt saw the need to help rural families survive by starting government programs, such as the Works Project Administration (WPA). One person from eligible families could work at such programs as were organized in the community. Dad worked on a road crew. They graveled roads with teams and wagons with loose planks for wagon beds. They shoveled the gravel on by hand and dumped their loads by tipping the planks on edge. A little slow by today's standards but everybody was glad for the small pay checks. As I remember, a man and team earned $45 per month. There were no power machines used. Even the graders were pulled with 4 or 6 horses.

Another government work program was the Civilian Conservation Corp. Wilmer was old enough to qualify then and he quit high school and joined. Their pay was $30 a month but the boys only got $5 of that and the rest was sent to the family which was a big help. They did some worthwhile conservation projects such as building dams and planting trees. They were sent to camps in various locations. Wilmer traveled to states such as South Dakota and Arkansas besides North Dakota.

The CCC boys built a good sized dam on Cedar creek about four or so miles from where we lived. It formed a lake that was big for that country and it is still used for recreation and also a small amount of irrigation. Wilmer worked on the construction of the dam.

It was a case of barely having enough money to survive. We had our own meat of course and there was milk, butter and eggs. Mother had a big garden but during the drought it was hard to raise much. Esther had worked her way though nurses training and had gotten a job as county nurse. Since that was a government job dad was no longer eligible for WPA. Esther helped out all during the depression. Wilmer did also.

Besides the lack of rainfall it seemed there were always grasshoppers. One year, I don't remember just what year it was but it must have been in the early 1930's, it was especially hot and dry that summer but we didn't have as many grasshoppers as usual. But one hot Sunday afternoon in midsummer we heard a strange noise and it suddenly became dark like a storm was coming. We looked out and saw the problem. It was a cloud of grasshoppers migrating from South Dakota where they had eaten everything they could.

First they were just flying over. They were so thick they actually blotted out the sun. Then they started to land. If there was anything green, like a weed or spear of grass, it would immediately be covered with hoppers. It didn't take long before they had devoured everything green and were looking for more. They sat on the shady side of wooden fence posts and on the side of buildings. They actually left noticeable pits on posts where they had been chewing. If some got inside the house, they chewed on the curtains. If you walked outside, they swarmed ahead of you. Some would fly up and hit you. If they flew up and hit you in the face, it was quite painful. Then one day they flew away as suddenly as they flew in. But not before they had destroyed everything that tried to grow that year.

One positive thing about it was the abundant feed for the turkeys and chickens. Even prairie chickens did well for a while.

I remember well the turkey harvest each year a little before Thanksgiving. These were free ranging turkeys. They would roam out about a half a mile from the place and always come back to roost at night. They were hatched under a hen and lived on grasshoppers and weed seeds until a couple weeks before they were killed. Then they were fed some corn to fatten them a little. On shipping day they were put in a small pen, stuck, hung up and the feathers pulled off. Then the naked birds were taken to the house where everyone in the family would pick pin feathers whether we wanted to or not. The pin feathers were little immature feathers that had to be picked one at a time. I had a definite dislike for turkey picking. The folks used to raise up to 150 birds a season.

After the birds were all picked clean they were packed—heads, guts and all—in wooden barrels. The lid was nailed down and then hauled to town to be shipped on the railroad to eastern markets.

The folks had rebuilt a herd of cattle and some sheep but there wasn't much of a market then. There was a fair market for work horses and Dad always had some for sale. That helped a lot, but buyers didn't always show up when they were needed. There were no auction barns yet. They were unheard of then.

We had good neighbors. Every one in the community got along. I can't remember anyone fighting or feuding in those days. If anyone needed help, the community was always there. The people worked together.

In 1937 the rains started to come back. Not too much in '37, but a little. The prairie grass had been dormant for so long it didn't recover right away so a lot of weeds came first and the grass eventually came back in subsequent years as the rains increased and were adequate for several years. We didn't have another dry year until 1949.

A little flicker of prosperity started to show up in 1938. The rains came and the farmers were raising crops again and the livestock had green grass. Another factor was that people were going back to work around the nation and were able to buy our produce again. Prices started to increase or at least there was a market for meat and grain. Before this I heard men talk about shipping cattle to Sioux City or St. Paul and the stock didn't sell for enough to pay the freight. Local markets hadn't been established yet so cattle and sheep had to be trailed to the railroad and loaded onto box cars to be shipped to big terminals, usually Sioux City, Iowa, St. Paul, Minnesota, or Chicago.

Usually the owner of the stock would accompany the shipment to make sure the animals were unloaded and fed about every 24 hours. Then when the shipment arrived at the destination, they would be consigned to a commission firm who would handle the sale. Auction barns have made marketing livestock much simpler and less expensive.

One convenience we had those early days was a telephone. I can't remember not having a phone. It was a wooden box on the wall with a little crank on the side. There were six or eight families on our line. If you wanted to call someone on your own line, you would first lift the receiver and see if anyone was already talking on the line. If it was clear, you would call the party you wanted to talk to by turning the crank to make a series of short and long rings. I still remember our signal was two short, a long and a short. Everyone on the line would hear the ring and anyone could (and often did) listen in or even talk.

Chapter 6

My Education

My education started when I was 5 years old (1929) and started the first grade at Washington School in Buena Vista township, northeast of Scranton, North Dakota. There were about 20 kids going to school there when I started. Ruby Benson was the teacher and she was great. She had to be to keep so many kids in line. I don't remember her having any problem with discipline. There were

Our country school.

more boys than girls so I imagine there was a little mischief going on, but nothing major.

Recess was a fun time with so many kids. We played a lot of different kinds of games.

One day the county superintendent came to visit. After he played the Star Spangled Banner on his saxophone, he gave us a little pep talk about school and then he asked us if we played ball at recess. We told him we didn't have a ball and bat. He said with so many boys we should have a ball team. So he gave us a ball and bat so we could play ball. We really appreciated that and we made good use of those gifts. We would choose teams and play ball. Russell Porten was the oldest and best athlete so he chose for one team. He always chose me to be on his team, which made me feel pretty important. There was no one to umpire the games but we didn't have many arguments. If we did, the bell would soon ring anyway and by the next recess everything would start fresh. Playing ball in grade school gave me enough experience so I was able to make the softball team in high school.

After I graduated from grade school at age 13, there was the problem of high school. My family wanted me to go to Augustana Academy - a boarding school for Lutherans at Canton, South Dakota. There I could work for part of my room, board and tuition, right at the school. Canton is located in extreme southeastern South Dakota, about 600 miles from home. I didn't want to go (back east) to school. No one rode horseback down there and I knew I couldn't spend the weekends hunting rabbits with my friend Johnnie Sipma. But I lost the argument and got on the train with my sister Shirla in the fall of 1938. She had been there for two years. My sister Esther had been the school nurse there at one time but had left to take a better paying job in Iowa.

Except for Shirla I didn't know anyone there and I was a green country kid. Actually that is an understatement. I had not been to town but a few times. Once a summer the Farmers Co-op in Scranton would have a picnic with free ice cream. Everyone would show up for that. Then each year we would get to go to town to get some new clothes to start school The dormitory at Augustana academy held about 90 boys so it wasn't long 'til I got acquainted and started to have a good time, though I missed having someone to talk to about horses. There were kids there from several different states and even some missionaries' kids from South Africa, but hardly any one from the west. I was no doubt boring, always wanting to talk about riding and ranching way out west. Then my sophomore year Wes Johnson, a ranch kid from the Rapid City area, came to school. His mother was the head cook at the school and she even had a car that Wes could drive on occasion. We got to be good friends and the next year we roomed together. He was only there

Old Main on the campus of Augustana Academy.

two years so I roomed with Ferdinand Jones (later known as Casey Jones). He was from Minnesota. His father was a road contractor. Ferdinand was a good athlete and also a talented singer. He later became a famous choir conductor in Denver, Colorado.

The first two years I was at the Academy I roomed with Gerhard (Johnnie) Johnson. He was a typical Norwegian boy from Minnesota so our background wasn't all that different. Although farming in Minnesota and ranching in western North Dakota are not the same but we were both from rural areas.

Most of the farm boys had jobs at the school. There were 8 acres of garden that had to be harvested after we got there in the fall plus a dairy operation and hogs to feed. Then there were dishes to wash in the cafeteria, janitor work in the class rooms and a huge coal furnace that operated the steam heat for the whole campus. Gerhard took great pride in taking care of the pigs. After every meal at the cafeteria he would haul a barrel of garbage to his pigs. It was a good thing he liked pigs because no one else wanted the job. I washed dishes all year and also worked in the garden in the fall. The boys that milked the cows had to get up about 4:30 or 5:00 to get the milking done and get back for 7:30 breakfast. That job was done by the Agrimson brothers and their cousins the Swiggum brothers, all from Minnesota.

I don't know if there was a minimum wage law then or not. I doubt it. We got 20 cents per hour and it was applied to our room and board. So that didn't get us any spending money for ourselves. So on our days off school we often went down the street knocking on doors to ask for odd jobs. Some people would not hire us but many did. I think a lot of people knew we were from the Academy and considered us charity cases.

We would clean basements, wash windows, shovel snow or maybe beat rugs. There were no vacuum cleaners yet so the rugs were hung on the clothes line and pounded with a rug beater or a stick until the dust was all gone.

One day Sumner Benson and I decided to go to downtown Canton and see if some business places would give us a little work. The first place we stopped was a hotel. The manager said we could clean his basement. We spent a couple hours at that and he paid us each 50 cents and gave us a noon meal. We thought the guy was all right.

After we ate we went to the K and K store. It was a small chain store where they sold both groceries and clothing. We talked to the manager and he said the kid that was the regular part time helper had just had his appendix out so he needed someone to take his place but he could only use one of us. Benson and I decided we would flip a coin to see who would stay and work. Benson won the toss but a few days later he decided to give up the job so I went to work in his place.

I learned a lot working there, knowledge that served me well when I ran my own store years later.

My first day on the job happened to be a Saturday. In those days Saturday night was the night the farmers came to town. Most of them brought a case of eggs in to trade for groceries. I had to learn how to candle eggs. There was a wooden box with two holes in the side just a little smaller than an egg and inside was a light bulb. Holding the egg up to the hole allows the light to shine through the egg and you can see if there is a dark spot in the yolk. If there is none, then the egg was fresh. If the yolk is dark colored or has dark spots on it, the egg is rejected.

There was no such thing as self serve stores then like it is now. People would come in with their lists and either read it to us or just hand the list to one of us and leave and come back later to pick up their items which we would have packed in a box ready for them. A lot of farmers would drop off their eggs and their grocery list on their way to the movie. After the movie we would be very busy as everyone would come in at the same time to pick up their groceries. This would be about 11:00 p.m. As soon as the movie crowd was taken care of and the doors were locked, we would fill shelves to be ready for Monday morning. Also all the fresh fruit and vegetables would be cleared from the bins and packed in boxes so that first thing Monday morning it would be sorted and only the fresh-looking produce would be put back on display. It was usually 3:00 a.m. Sunday morning before we could leave. It sure made for a long day.

I worked there from late fall until spring. When softball season started, I quit. Being my senior year I would have missed a lot of activities.

The experience was good and the pay was average for the time. I worked about 32 hours a week for $6. By today's standards that is pretty puny. Social Security had not been operating very long then. They deducted 6 cents from my paycheck and the company matched it. That's pretty funny when you think of it now. Workman's Comp. had not been thought of yet.

I still remember some of the prices of a few items. Coffee was 21 cents a pound. A loaf of bread from the local bakery was 9 cents. A loaf of Sweetheart bread was 12 cents. A little sack of candy was 1 penny. A pound of minced ham was 21 cents. We also sold dry goods. A pair of shoes was $4 to $5 for the best. A good top coat was $18 and up.

You could buy a hamburger in a restaurant for a nickel and a bottle of pop was the same. A full meal cost 25 cents. I didn't drink beer those days but I believe a glass of beer was a nickel. Times have changed, haven't they? At these prices maybe my part time job for $6 a week wasn't so bad after all. The store manager offered me a steady job after I graduated for $35 a month but I wanted to get back west where cowboys weren't such a curiosity. Horses have become popular back there now but in those days there were none except work horses on the farms. The farmers in that area raised a lot of corn and it was picked by hand. A team pulling a wagon would walk down the corn rows while the picker would snap off the corn cobs and toss them in the wagon. It was interesting to watch the horses start and stop as the picker spoke to them, always going straight down the rows. It was a slow process by today's standards but it gave jobs to a lot of men. They were mostly transients.

The academy was built less than a half mile from the Big Sioux River. That furnished us with a good place to ice skate in the winter. Ice skating was a popular form of entertainment those days and I think almost everyone in both the girls' and boys' dorms had a pair of skates. On Sunday afternoons we would pick up some girls at the girls' dorm and hike down to the river to ice skate. If it was cold out we would build a bonfire. We thought it was great fun and it didn't cost anything. That was important because none of us had any extra money to spend just for fun.

With all the activities and sports available at school, it was hard for me to concentrate on my studies. I thought there was no hurry, I could get serious later. My grades reflected my attitude. It wasn't that school was hard for me. It was just hard for me to focus on studying when there was so much fun to be had. Finally the last half of my senior year something convinced me to take a more mature attitude toward education and I actually started to open the books and my grades improved. Who knows what would have happened if I had pursued a college education.

In 1952 I went to my ten year class reunion. There was one person there who had graduated sixty years previous. I thought that was pretty remarkable to have lived that long. In 2002 Rose Marie and I went to my sixty year reunion and there were fourteen of us there. Not bad for a class of forty five.

Chapter 7
Moved To Amidon

I had just turned seventeen and was a senior at the Academy when the Japanese attacked Pearl Harbor. It was a Sunday morning when we heard the news. We were getting ready to go to church. Everyone had his radio on to the news but I don't think reality set in for several days but we knew that it wouldn't be long until several of us would be in the armed services. Some acted eager to go and others were not. At seventeen I was still too young to go. I went home after graduation.

Wilmer was called soon after the start of the war and the draft board said I was to stay home and help run the ranch. That didn't bother me even though

My High School graduation photo

several of my buddies enlisted. When I did get called to take the physical I took the train to Fort Snelling Minnesota. I remember some of the guys that went the same day. There was Kenneth Spethman, Don Howie, Winfield Austin and some fellows from Hardin County, South Dakota. I believe John R. Olson was with us and I don't remember the rest. After sixty years a person is liable to forget some details. I passed the physical and waited for a call to be inducted but my number didn't come up until the war was over so I didn't have to go. I didn't ask to stay home but I didn't volunteer either. The folks would have had a hard time alone. Even though Dad was in good health for his age, he was nearly 70 years old at the time. The country needed agriculture products, too. I also had a selfish motive for staying home. I had a steady girl friend. But that turned out to be a temporary situation.

Wilmer was a radio operator and received a purple heart in Germany. When the conflict was over in Europe, he was sent to the Philippines until the Japanese surrendered and the war was over. We were glad to have him back and all the rest of the service men and women. I believe right after World War II was the best time the U.S. has ever seen. It was

Mother and Dad in their working clothes.

peacetime and people were employed. Wages were higher than they had been before the war and inflation hadn't become a problem yet. Wheat was selling good. In fact, during the Korean War it jumped to $3.00 a bushel. Beef prices were rising. Steer calves would soon be 20 cents.

In 1940 the folks decided to leave the Scranton area. It was getting harder and harder to find range to run livestock there. Farmers were buying up the land and breaking up the sod to raise grain, mostly wheat. Dad found a place 4 miles west of Amidon, North Dakota, that suited him better. There was a spring fed creek and better winter protection. They rented the place for a couple years and eventually bought it. I was away at school when they moved. Wilmer and a neighbor—Harry Norby—trailed the range horses to the new place but I believe the cattle were trucked.

The folks lived on that place until dad died at age 84 and mother lived with Shirla for a few years after that. She later moved to Park Ridge, Illinois. near Chicago where Esther was working as a Deaconess in the Lutheran Deaconess Hospital. Mother passed away there at age 91. She was buried beside Dad at Amidon.

Moving to Amidon meant leaving the old neighborhood and friends but it wasn't like moving far away. We would see old friends from time to time in town and at special occasions like weddings, funerals and anniversaries. There were new friends to make at Amidon. We found good neighbors there and it didn't take long to make new friends. I would go back to South Dakota during the school year until I graduated in 1942.

The summer after graduation a classmate from South Dakota, Sumner Benson, came out to spend the summer with me. He had never spent time on a ranch before but he was a fast learner. He learned to ride quickly and was good help with haying and fencing or whatever we happened to be doing.

I took a job that summer measuring fields for the government farm program. It was called the Agriculture Adjustment Act, (AAA.) The government would pay farmers to leave land idle or to strip crop where they divided their fields into strips of various widths, quite often 10 rods wide. Every other strip would be summer fallowed. This method was designed to reduce wind erosion which was such a problem during the dirty 30's. My job was to measure all the fields in two townships in the southeast corner of Slope County. They were Cedar Creek and Woodbury townships. I was well acquainted in that area, having lived just across the county line in Bowman County.

We measured with a 100 ft. tape and a set of pins with a loop on one end so I needed a helper. Once again Benson was there to handle the other end of the tape. It was a lot of walking. While we were measuring, I would draw a sketch of each field and record the measurements. Then when we finished measuring each farm, I would draw the fields on aerial maps and write in the measurements so the acreage could be calculated in the AAA office at the court house in Amidon.

It was a pretty good job but we finished in about a month so it didn't last long. I don't remember what I got paid but I imagine it was pretty good for those days.

Later that fall I helped some of the neighbors thresh. Threshing was still fairly common then. It wasn't many years later when harvesting grain was all done with combines. Some farmers that had livestock would combine their wheat and then thresh their oats and barley so they could have a straw pile for livestock feed.

Threshing was much more labor intensive than combining. First the grain had to be cut with a binder which tied the stalks into bundles and dumped in windrows. Then someone had to walk down the windrows and set the bundles up in a teepee fashion with the grain heads pointing up. This was called shocking and would keep the heads off the ground so the grain would dry without sprouting if it got rained on. If the grain sprouted, it was no good for anything but livestock feed. If it was put in a granary, it would mold and possibly even ignite and burn. When the grain was all shocked, it was time to start threshing. Not every farmer had a threshing machine. Those that did would organize the neighborhood and those with grain to thresh would get together to make up a crew. The size of the machine determined the size of the crew. A small machine would only need 3 teams of horses with hay racks while the big ones could keep 10 teams busy. The men driving the teams would have to drive out in the field and pitch on all the bundles he could get on the rack and then drive up to the machine, sometimes called a separator, and pitch it off one at a time being careful not to pitch too fast for fear of plugging the machine and causing down time. If the bundle haulers thought they needed a little rest, they could purposely plug the machine by pitching more than one bundle at a time or putting some in crosswise. Plugging the machine would make the machine tender quite upset. Hauling bundles was work from daylight 'til dark and it was hot and dusty but there were exciting times, too. If a bundle hauler loaded one side too heavy, the rack could tip over and then of course animals are not always predictable and because there would be no one holding the lines as the teams went down the windrows, they could run away if something spooked them. If one team took off and ran, there was a good chance another team would follow suit. Then there were rattlesnakes to watch out for. They would go under the shocks hunting for mice and then go to sleep there. They would be pretty bad tempered when they lost their quiet shelter.

But the best part was the good food that was served. The men expected three big meals every day and coffee and sandwiches to be brought out to the field about midmorning and again in the afternoon. I think the women who cooked had it harder than the men. In the early days they didn't have modern conveniences. Imagine cooking three big meals every day for up to 20 men with meat, mashed potatoes, vegetables, and always pie for dessert with no refrigeration or electricity. There was no running to the store for fresh produce and of course bread had to be baked. All on a wood or coal stove. Times have changed for the better in some things. I'm sure farmers' wives will agree with that. It was impossible for one person to do all the cooking, so neighbor ladies would help each other. By the late 1940's shock threshing was pretty much a thing of the past.

A few farms and ranches had their own electric plants before President F.D.R. established the R.E.A. and brought electricity to rural folks. But most of them didn't. It took several years before the lines reached remote areas like Amidon, North Dakota, and Roosevelt was long dead before we saw the bright lights come to our country. We were hooked up in the summer of 1948. I remember well the day it happened. I came home after dark that day and when I drove into the yard, Mother had every light in the house on. Believe me it was quite a contrast with the old kerosene lamps we used before the miracle of electricity.

Now we could have a refrigerator instead of the ice box. The old Maytag washing machine with the smoky old gas engine could be discarded and best of all, we could have a bath instead of a path. Life was great. We could now have things that city folks took for granted.

Putting up ice for the ice box was a miserable job. I am certainly glad we don't have to do that any more. It was usually done in February before the weather got too warm. It was best if the temperature was at 0 degrees or colder so that the ice cake would be frozen dry when they were pulled out of the water. We would drive out on a pond or lake and cut cakes of ice about 2 feet square (with an ice saw) and however thick the ice was. It would vary from year to year but I think it would average about 2 feet thick. After the cakes were cut, tongs were attached and the cake was lifted out of the water and slid up a ramp into a truck and hauled to the ice house where it was packed in sawdust. It would keep from thawing all summer if it was covered properly. Then at least once a day a cake of ice had to be brought in for the ice box. That was a nuisance, too. The refrigerator is a better system.

During the drought and depression of the 1930's there was a lot of land abandoned in southwestern North Dakota. People had no money to pay the taxes so the counties took ownership. If the land had been farmed, it had been left idle long enough so it grew back to grass after the rains came again. This land became known as tax title land because the county took title because of delinquent taxes. The former owners could redeem the land within 7 years by paying the back taxes and penalties but very few did. There wasn't much interest in owning land for several years after the depression.

County-wide auctions were held and some of the land would be sold. The land was previously appraised and that would be the minimum bid. If it wasn't sold then, it would be held until the following year. Dad was able to buy some good grazing land for as little as $2.00 an acre. I'm sure later on he wished he would have bought more. Our county commissioners set aside some of the tax title land for service men so they could buy some land when they got back. Brother Wilmer was able to take advantage of that and got a little start when he got back from the war.

We had a band of sheep. Wilmer also had a small band. When he went to the army, he left them for me to take care of. During the war it was hard to find sheep shearers so the extension service held a sheep shearing school in Bowman. Shearers were charging 25¢ a head if you could find a crew. So I decided I'd take advantage of the opportunity. I went to the two day school and learned to shear sheep. I was able to buy a used shearing machine with a gasoline engine and was ready to make my fortune shearing sheep. Good shearers could shear 100 or more head a day. At 25¢ a head it sounded better than any kind of labor for $5 a day. There was one little detail I had overlooked. As the old saying goes, it takes a strong back and a weak mind to do certain things and shearing sheep is one of those things. I'm fairly tall so it was a long way to bend over. By the end of the day my back would hurt like you couldn't believe. I toughed it out for 3 seasons but never got fast enough to do 100 head a day. I finally decided my career as a sheep shearer wasn't going to make me rich so I sold my outfit to a Mexican and quit.

Chapter 8

Trucking & Trailing

My next endeavor was to be a trucker. You might say I was following in my father's footsteps being a freighter but I had a few more horsepower then he did. In those days not too many ranchers and farmers had their own trucks so there was a demand for truckers to haul grain, livestock and coal (most people heated their homes with coal). It seemed like a good idea because I could help at the ranch and do some trucking when I had time. It turned out just the opposite. I did some trucking and helped Dad with the ranch when I had time.

There were no new trucks available because of the war and not many used ones on the market either. The ones being sold were bringing black market prices. I found a 1937 Ford 1 1/2 ton truck owned by Norman Wolfgram who was a commercial trucker and he was upgrading to a little newer one. I borrowed $750 and bought the six year old truck. You might say the truck had quite a bit of experience. I paid him in cash because the price control agency said the truck was worth $450. Looking back that wasn't much money but it seemed it took a long time to pay it off. In 1937, Ford had not started to make vehicles with hydraulic brakes or sealed beam headlights. If you drove 45 m.p.h. at night you were overdriving the headlights, but you probably had to have a little down slope to reach a speed of 45 m.p.h. anyway, especially if you were loaded.

By today's standards it wasn't much of a truck but it had a pretty good 14 ft. box and stock rack and I was in business. It didn't have a very good heater and even if it would have had a radio, I would not have been able to hear it above the noise of the motor.

At first I just hauled pretty much locally. I could haul 165 bushels of wheat and I got 7¢ a bushel. I had to shovel the grain on by hand and if I started at sunup I could make three trips a day if it wasn't much over 30 miles one way. So if I put in a 14 hour day and things went well I could make $35 a day. We didn't mind working hard because we didn't know any difference and gas was cheap. There were no portable elevators or augers then. After a couple of years I got the idea to build a small elevator that I could carry with me. It was powered with a Briggs & Stratton engine. I thought I was pretty clever. No one else had one. It wasn't too long before the Mayrath Company came out with an auger mounted on a set of wheels and that revolutionized the way we loaded grain. I don't know why it took so long for someone to think of building an auger. Anyway it was a great improvement.

I hauled quite a lot of livestock those days. With that first little truck I could haul 10 cows or 20 calves. I charged 40¢ a loaded mile. Cows were smaller those days. A big cow might weigh 1000 lbs. and not many calves weighed over 350 lbs. at weaning time.

Hauling livestock was easier on the back but harder on the nerves. The roads out to ranches those days were not much better than a couple ruts across the country and sometimes it would be so sidling I was sure I would tip over when the load would shift to the downhill side. There were some hills coming out of the badlands that were so steep a single axle truck would rear up off the ground in front so we would have to have an empty truck chained to the front of the loaded one. One such hill was coming from the Logging Camp Ranch on the Little Missouri River west of Amidon.

The early day truck and trailer semis couldn't make it without help either because of lack of power. The big diesel powered trucks on the road nowdays can pull the hills without any trouble I'm sure. Besides better trucks now the roads have been much improved.

There were still quite a few semi-wild horses in the country and the market for killer horses was starting to pick up. If someone had quite a few to go, I would get the job to trail them to town. I would have a couple riders to help, of course. If there were just a truck load to go, then I would haul them. Not all truckers would haul wild horses because they were hard on equipment. The first load I hauled was a load of especially wild ones and I no more than got away from the loading chute when one big gelding jumped over the side. In doing so he broke the top two boards off my stock rack. The horse wasn't hurt, but that left a possible escape for the rest of the load. I happened to have some rope along and I tied that across the hole several times. I was glad to get to Dickinson where I unloaded, feeling lucky to have gotten there short only one horse.

I mentioned trailing horses. It was about 1946 or so when a buyer bought about 30 heard of horses from some neighbors. It was in the spring and it happened there were seven studs to go and of course each one thought he should have a little band of mares of his own and didn't want to stay with the others. These were not herd sires but young studs that had not yet been gelded. It was quite a challenge to keep the herd bunched up at first but I had my buddy Curt Homelvig with me, as was the usual case, and the buyer sent two kids out from town. After 4 or 5 miles, we had pretty good control so one rider could go in the lead and the herd would line out behind him. We were headed for New England, about 30 miles from where we started.

Some time in the afternoon we were going along making pretty good time. One of the New England guys was in the lead when I noticed the herd made a little split around something and I couldn't see Johnnie. When the horses got past what they were dodging, our boy was picking himself up from under his saddle. His latigo had broken and the saddle turned and when he fell off, he slipped the bridle off, too. I don't know how, but he did.

We held up the herd then and because the horse that got away was pretty tired by then, we roped another one that had saddle marks on his back and we were pretty sure he could be ridden the rest of the way. The horse turned out to be good enough and we patched the broken latigo with one of the saddle strings.

We didn't have any more trouble until we got to the bridge over the Cannon Ball River just outside of New England. It was just starting to get dark. We had timed ourselves about right. We had stopped to rest the horses about 10 miles out and we thought we had enough time. I was in the lead then and the road looked clear to cross the bridge, but just as I started to cross, a car turned onto the road off a side street and was about to cross the bridge. I waved to try to get the driver to back off but instead he turned on his lights and proceeded to come across. That scattered the horses some but because they were pretty tired and pretty well trail broke by then, they didn't give us much trouble until we tried to get them to step onto the bridge. They flat refused to follow me across. I managed to catch the horse Johnnie had fallen off of and he led across and the rest followed. The corral where we were going to was just beyond the bridge so we got them in before it got completely dark. They would be loaded on railroad boxcars to be shipped to Missouri. Most of the horses on that trip belonged to Elmer Mack and he had sold them to Fred Schatz, a buyer, in New England. Elmer brought us some lunch about noon so we held up the herd and gave them a rest while we had a lunch of beer, cheese and crackers.

A little later that spring I took the job to trail another bunch for the same buyer. This time we started from the Art Spethman ranch, about a 40 mile trip. Curt helped me again and also Russ Alexander and his cousin, also an Alexander. I can't remember his first name. Those two were about 12 years old and pretty eager to go. I don't remember much happening on that trip that would be worth telling.

I helped trail horses to Bowman a couple of times, too, once with Bill Hill and once with Curt Homelvig and Bruce Lambourn. We went around the west side of Black Butte to avoid traffic which made it a few miles further. Probably about 30 miles total. We came back home the next day. The fall of 1949 Russ Alexander, Blackie Hodecek and I trailed 2 carloads of steers to Bowman for Elmer Mack.

The Schmidt Brothers had a ranch on the west end of Black Butte. They had a large band of sheep and a small bunch of goats. As we passed the goats, a big billy decided to come with us. Now billie goats are famous for their foul odor. I mean really foul. To make matters worse we were driving into the wind. I cut him back and drove him towards home a couple times but he would just turn around and soon be up with the cattle again. By that time we had come several miles and we were getting pretty tired of the smell. In desperation I roped the goat and tied him down with a pickin string and left him there. We didn't make it to town that night with the herd but when we stopped that night Elmer took me back to the goat and I turned him loose. I thought he would find his way back home. But instead he wandered into Jr. Burkes' place. When I saw Jr. in town a few days later he had a few choice names to call me. He was good natured about it though. (I think.)

Max Wilson was leasing the Gress ranch which was originally the George Clark ranch where the good cowboy Elmer Clark grew up. It was located north of Amidon I would guess about 10 miles. One fall John Gerbig and I helped Max trail some yearling steers to Medora. That was a three day drive and a beautiful ride. We followed the Little Missouri River all the way so we were in the badlands and crossed the river several times. The cattle could graze along the way and could drink out of the river whenever they wanted to. The river is usually quite low at that time of the year so crossing it was no problem.

The first night we made it to Ray Pasch's ranch. Ray was a widower. His wife had been killed in a car accident. He had 2 small children, a boy and a girl. Ray was a good cook and since we had been riding since daylight with nothing to eat since breakfast, the steaks he fixed were really appreciated. Then for dessert he whipped up an angel food cake. He was well known in the community for his angel food cakes. There were no box mixes those days but that didn't bother Ray.

The second day we made it to Walt Christianson's Custer Trail Ranch. This was the location of the first dude ranch in the country. It was established by the Eaton Brothers who later moved their operation to Sheridan, Wyoming. We enjoyed the good old western hospitality at the Christianson ranch for ourselves and our horses as well.

The next day was a short trip but we had to graze the cattle on the river bottom until late in the afternoon before the railroad was ready to load. When the rail cars were spotted at the loading chute, we loaded the cattle and they were on the way to St. Paul. John rode home that night so he could help his brother Morris who was starting out with a herd of 2 year old steers the next day. Max and I stayed in the original Rough Riders Hotel that night and rode home the next day.

I didn't help trail much stock to town after that. For one thing I had gotten a semi trailer and was expanding my trucking business. Then, too, there was some sale barns starting up around the country. Schnells in Dickinson was the first one in our part of the state. Later Bill Haman and a couple partners built the Western Livestock Co. also in Dickinson. Then George Remelong started one in the old railroad stock yards in Bowman. Shortly after that Bill Carter built a yard over the site where we used to play baseball. He called it the Home Base Auction Co. because the office was directly over what was home base. There wasn't enough business for two yards in Bowman so Carter bought Remelong out and did well for many years. When he retired, he sold out to Bob Penfield who is an auctioneer.

I stayed in the trucking business for six years. It was a fun business to be in for a young single fellow, but it was also scary at times.

One day my neighbor Burke Lambourn asked me to haul his threshing machine from his father-in-law, Charley Bahm's place to his place. I would guess it to be about 20 miles over some pretty rough country. This machine was at least 10 ft. tall and at that time I just had the little 1 1/2 ton Ford truck. I told him I was afraid to haul something that top heavy over those roads. He said he thought we could make it all right if we drove slow. I thought it over and decided I would give it a try. I would drive so slow that if I did tip over, I wouldn't hurt much on the truck and Burke was willing to take a chance so we went to get it. It was parked out on the prairie about 1/2 mile from any kind of a road. We found a little bank that I could back up to so we could pull the machine onto the truck bed. When we got it on the truck and chained down, it made my little truck look like a toy. To get to the road I drove as slow as I possibly could and picked my way so as not to go anywhere it would be at all sidling. When we got to the country road that would take us to Burke's we had no choice but to go straight down the road.

This was just a dirt road with lots of chuck holes. If the chuck holes were equal on each track, it wasn't so bad, but if there was a hole on just one track, it made it pretty tippy. I would almost come to a stop and let the wheels drop into the hole. The load would sway over to one side and just about the time I expected it was going over, it would sway back the other way. And I would goose it a little and we'd come out of that one and drive on to the next one. It was a nerve racking trip but we made it.

I hauled another threshing machine later that fall. That one was for Frued Williams. But that was on better roads and I made it ok.

Nowadays truckers haul big combines and go from Texas to Canada and back but they have a lot bigger trucks and good highways. In 1947 I bought a new Federal truck. It was much bigger than the little Ford I started out with. The tires were 9.00 x 20 as compared to 7.00 x 20 on the little Ford which allowed me to haul 250 bushels of wheat instead of 165 bushels. This truck was big enough to pull a semi which I did later on.

I made several trips to West Fargo with livestock and also a few trips to South St. Paul and Sioux City. One trip to West Fargo stands out in my memory. It was winter and there was quite a bit of snow. In those

My two trucks in 1949.

days the highways went through the middle of towns instead of bypassing them as they do now. Highway 10 went through Jamestown, North Dakota, and when you were east bound, you had to make a sharp turn and immediately start up a fairly steep and fairly long hill. Since the turn was so sharp, there was no way to get a run at the hill. This night there was ice on the east bound lane but the west bound lane was bare. I no more than started up the hill already in first gear I started to spin out. There was no chance I was going to make the hill in my lane without chaining up so I put on my hazard lights and pulled over in the left lane and went on up the hill. I met some cars but since this was in the city limits, everyone was driving slow and they had time to think and they all turned out and went around me on the wrong side. I was glad when I made it to the top of the hill. I was also glad I didn't meet any highway patrolmen.

In the fall and early winter there was a lot of coal to haul. That was hard work but some one had to do it. This was during the 1940s and I was young and I thought I was tough. We had trouble finding a coal mine that could load us when we wanted. There were several mines within a two hour drive from Amidon but they were all short of men and equipment. We would have to arrive at the loading site very early in the morning in order to be in line to get loaded that day. Most mines had a small scale house that was heated so we could stay warm while we waited.

One day I went to Regent, North Dakota, to get a load. There I found a friend from Bowman who was also waiting to get loaded. My load was to go to Bowman that day too so we decided to travel together in case one of us had trouble. He said he knew a short cut so he would lead the way. It was dark when we left the mine. Bill led us on a gravel road, (all the good roads were gravel then), which soon became a dirt road which became nothing more than a trail. It was obvious we were lost but we had no way of communicating. There were no C.B.s then.

We came to a long, fairly steep hill which required using lower and lower gears. We were making it up the hill but very slowly. All of a sudden Bills' truck stopped moving forward and started to roll back down the hill toward me. I was about 100 yards behind him. I stopped and put my truck in reverse and hoped I could back straight enough in the dark to stay on the road. I assumed Bill had broken an axle so that he couldn't use his gears to hold the truck from rolling back. Trucks those days didn't have very good brakes but by using both the brake pedal and the emergency brake he was able to get his truck stopped. I quickly stopped my truck and ran up and got a big lump of coal from his load to block the wheel. I had guessed right. He had a broken axle. So we left his truck there and he rode in with me.

He admitted we were lost and didn't know where we were. We were looking for highway 12, (formerly called The Yellowstone Trail.) So we kept going south or west whatever looked best. When we finally found highway 12 we were at Hettinger, North Dakota. We were considerably further east than we intended but we were glad to know where we were. The bright lights of Hettinger were a welcome sight.

Lud Olson was a big tall Norwegian and a real nice guy. He lived east of Amidon. I hauled cattle for him at different times. Once he made arrangements for me to haul a load of bred dairy heifers from the little town of Chetek, Wisconsin. Lud had a brother there and he picked up this load of heifers. Lud resold them around Amidon one or two at a time. Amidon wasn't a dairy country but most people had a milk cow or maybe 3 or 4. I doubt if that's the case anymore though I couldn't say for sure as I left Amidon over 45 years ago. I think most people get their milk at the friendly grocery store.

I found out it gets cold in Wisconsin. This was February and there was lots of snow. Luds' brother (I can't remember his first name) met me in town and we went to the stock yards to look at the heifers. They were nice heifers but one looked like she could calve any time. The man in charge of the stockyards asked me what kind of truck I was driving. I told him it was a brand new Federal. Then he said, "You had better park it so I can give you a pull in the morning. It's going to get cold tonight and your truck won't start in the morning." (The engine block heater hadn't been invented yet.) I told him I appreciated the offer but I planned to start out at 4:00 a.m. He said that was no problem for him.

Mr. Olson took me home to his farm and after the milking was done, we had a wonderful supper, cooked by his wonderful Norwegian wife. After supper Mr. Olson said, "I want to take you to town and show you off to the boys." There were seven beer parlors in that little town and I had to meet the boys at each one. Because I came from the west, I was quite a celebrity. Since I wanted to get an early start, we didn't stay out late but I really enjoyed the hospitality. The next morning the thermometer at Olson's farm said 30 below. The man at the stock yards was right—it got cold. He was at the yard when Mr. Olson brought me in. He gave me a pull to get the truck running and then helped me load. I tried to pay him for his trouble but he wouldn't take anything. He said, "You probably won't ever get a chance to help me, but help someone else." That remark made an impression on me and I've never forgotten it.

It was too long a trip for the heifers to make it back to Amidon in one day so I stopped at Long Prairie, Minnesota, to give them and me, a rest. Shirla and Howard were farming there at the time so I unloaded at their place. Next morning it was even colder, at 40 below. Howard had a tractor in the barn with his cows all night so he gave me a pull. To make matters worse the close up heifer was starting to go into labor. I borrowed a panel from Howard and put her in a corner and hoped she would hold out till I got to Amidon. It was a miracle but when I got to Lud Olson's that night, she was still on her feet with one of the calf's feet showing. Lud pulled the calf and everything was fine. The calf was still alive.

At that time in my life I had never seen an ocean, so when I got a load of furniture to haul from Dickinson, North Dakota, to Portland, Oregon, I decided I'd go to see the Pacific. My friend Curt Homelvig was with me on that trip and we enjoyed the scenery. When we got unloaded in Portland, we took off to see the big pond. We were disappointed. The beach was loaded with trash of all kinds that had washed up on shore. We hadn't taken into account that it was winter and nobody much cared about the beach. Besides it just happened to be a cold windy day. So we turned around and started for home. On the way back we stopped at Seeley Lake at a saw mill and picked up a load of rough lumber for a back haul.

On the way out to Portland my truck developed a bad noise in the differential after we had only gone a couple hundred miles. I stopped in Billings, Montana, and had it checked out and they found a badly chipped cog in the ring gear. It would not have been prudent to go any further. There wasn't a new ring gear for that model truck closer than Denver. We thought we were doomed to stay for a few days while we waited for parts. This was on Monday afternoon. The parts were shipped air freight overnight and by 11:00 a.m. Tuesday we were on the road. That was mighty good service by the boys at Motor Power and Equipment Co., a company dealing only in big trucks. I don't remember what the total bill was, but I remember the freight from Denver was $5.00, considerably less than it would be today. That was the fall of 1948.

North and South Dakota had a bumper crop of wheat and also flax in 1948. I anticipated a good business hauling grain that fall so I decided to buy another truck. Trucks were still hard to find as factories weren't fully converted to peacetime manufacturing yet. I found a dealer in Belle Fourche, South Dakota, who said he could get me a new Chevy for $2800 and it would be there in 2 weeks. He called 10 days later and said my truck was on its way from Ohio and I could come and get it. On the day he assured me it would be there, I hitch-hiked to Belle Fourche to drive the new truck home. When I got there the truck wasn't there and we found out the driver had been bribed somewhere along the way so it wasn't going to ever arrive.

I had made some commitments and really needed the second truck. It happened the dealer I'd been talking to had a 1947 K5 International truck on his lot with 10,000 miles on it so I bought it for $2400 and went on my way. That turned out to be one of the most dependable vehicles I ever owned so everything worked out all right, as it usually does.

One day shortly before harvest I was coming back from a trip to Gillette, Wyoming, and I stopped at

Buffalo, South Dakota, for supper. I got to visiting with a stranger who turned out to be looking for a couple trucks to haul flax. His name was Al Johnson from Deadwood, South Dakota. He and two others were in partnership on a whole section of flax west of Buffalo at Harding. I took the job and hired Earl, (Pud) Inman from Amidon to drive one truck. We kept a room at the hotel in Buffalo and also had a camp at Harding. We were kept busy keeping the grain away from the combine. The railroad couldn't keep enough boxcars at the elevators to make room for the grain that was coming in. We kept calling elevators in the area to see who had room for flax. We hauled to Belle Fourche and Newell in South Dakota and Bowman, North Dakota. Flax was a good price in 1948. It was selling between $5.50 and $6.00 a bushel.

Belle Fourche was a 75 mile haul, Newell almost that far and Bowman was 50 miles so it was a good job for me. We hauled for 2 weeks without stopping.

Al Johnson was of Finnish descent and proud of it. He was an interesting guy who had been places and done things and was a great story teller. He had worked in the mines in Butte, Montana, been a champion sheep shearer, a cowboy, and a heavy equipment operator. He also enjoyed a beer now and then. You couldn't help but like the guy. I don't remember the names of the other two fellows who were in on the deal. One was quite religious and wouldn't take a drink, but he brought out watermelons by the dozen. He liked to share his melons with anyone who would eat with him. He could eat a whole melon and sometimes two all by himself. The third partner was a well known gambler. It was interesting around camp.

There was still a lot of virgin sod in the country and with the high price of flax in 1948, a lot of sod was plowed up and planted to flax. Flax does well on new breaking. For one thing, it usually doesn't have to compete with weeds. (There wasn't such a thing as herbicides those days.) That spring a neighbor, Bill Hill, asked me if I wanted to break some ground and plant flax for him on shares. I had hardly any equipment then but I said I would. Wilmer had some ground suitable for breaking, too. I went to town and bought an old 2236 International tractor from Link Flados at Stuber Implement. It was an antique tractor but it ran well and had been converted from steel wheels to rubber tires and it would pull 3 breaker bottoms. Wilmer bought a plow and we were in business. Neither of us was very experienced in farming but the rains came and we had a good crop. I'd rather be lucky than good.

I had a 2 year lease with Bill Hill and the plan was to seed the ground to wheat the second year which was the usual practice. The problem was that year it didn't rain and the wheat made 5 bushel per acre. The landlord got 1/3 for his share so we hardly made expenses and we donated our time. Our luck ran out. Well, I never claimed to be a farmer anyway. I thought we were lucky to get one good crop. I always had more faith in livestock than grain farming. Some people have made good money raising small grain in this country but you need good equipment and the expertise to do the job right.

The winter of 1949 was one for the record books. I was coming back from a trip to Fargo with the semi when the first storm of the season hit. I made it home but just barely about midnight on Jan 1st. The next morning the roads were blocked and stayed blocked for 6 weeks.

I was obligated to make payments on the rig every 2 weeks and I needed to be on the road. I had hauling lined up but couldn't move. The finance company started to write nasty letters but I couldn't do anything about it. I was frustrated and helpless. Finally after 6 weeks I got going. I wrote the finance company and explained I was hauling again and would be sending a check soon.

But my troubles weren't over yet. I had hauled 5,000 bushels. of wheat for one man and he paid me with a check. He was a fairly big farmer-rancher and well respected in the community. I was surprised when his check bounced. Of course as soon as I deposited his check, I sent one of mine to the finance company which also bounced and that really irritated them. I received a telegram in a couple days saying they were starting a procedure to foreclose on my truck. I wasn't worried the guy wouldn't make the check good. I just didn't know if we could get it done soon enough. As soon as I was sure I had the money, I sent a telegram explaining the facts and please stop the foreclosure and they did. That was close.

That was a miserable winter, one of the few I remember. The snow was deep, the wind blew every day except 3 during the month of January and it was bitter cold. Some days it didn't get above 30 below, and there was quite a bit of death loss among livestock. The snow drifted so hard the horses could walk on top sometimes and then they would fall through so it was hard going. I rode horse back to Amidon a few times to get the mail and a few groceries. The neighbors rode too or drove a team.

The neighbors to the north had three boys. Buster was my age and Clarence was a little younger and Bumps was the youngest. They were the Roland Miller family. One Saturday night Clarence called me and said Bud Mack was going to ride up to their place and why don't I come up too and we would play some cards. I guess we were feeling sorry for ourselves since we couldn't get out to go to town for Saturday night. It was a bitter cold night but there was no wind and the moon was shining bright. So I dressed for the occasion and saddled up. It was about two miles from our place to Millers and the snow was at least two feet deep so it was hard work for the horses. It was probably midnight when Bud and I decided it was time to go home. When I got home I looked at the thermometer to find it was an even 30 degrees below zero.

Finally in February the National Guard sent out a fleet of caterpillars with dozers and they broke the roads out so we could at least get to town. Some of the drifts were eight or ten feet deep. They just made a track wide enough to drive a car through so you didn't want to have to meet anyone.

Toward the end of February it turned warm and the snow melted fast. The water all went down the creeks before the ground thawed out so all that snow didn't do us much good. The spring that year was cold and windy and dry. It was so dry that the grass didn't get green. It stayed dry all summer. If it would not have been for the wet year we had the previous year and a lot of old grass remained, I'm sure ranchers would have had to sell down their herds. Some people even cut the year old grass for hay. The winter of 1950 which followed was an open one so we survived with the old grass and a little cake.

Chapter 9

The Mack Ranch

In the fall of 1949 our neighbor Elmer Mack said he wanted to sell us his ranch. It bordered Dad's for 2½ miles on the west and would work well together. It was a good grass ranch, very well watered by a spring fed creek (Sand Creek) and there was adequate winter protection. It would be a dream come true. I would quit trucking and be a full time rancher. I liked trucking but by then I was ready to quit. From the time I was little, my goal was always to someday own a ranch. I told Elmer that if I could find the financing, I would surely buy it. He said he would buy my semi so he could set his son Elmer Jr. up in the trucking business. Elmer Jr. was my age and a good friend. We called him Bud.

The Mack ranch is a historical site and is the scene of a fight between a small band of Indians and three men who were tending a station on the stage coach route between Fort Lincoln near Mandan, North Dakota, and Fort Keogh near Miles City, Montana. The story was told to me by "Doc" Alexander whose brother "Ab", had owned the ranch before Elmer Mack became the owner. The story was also researched and written up in a book by Father Louis Pfaller of the Assumption Abby in Richardton, North Dakota, in 1954. Father Pfaller came to the ranch while he was doing his research and Wilmer and I got to talk with him.

The story goes something like this.—The stage had just left after changing horses. The tired horses were turned out to graze. When some Indians came to run the horses off the three men tried to stop them. The Indians shot and killed two of them and the third man managed to catch a mule and rode bareback to Medora to tell of the incident. Frank Roberts, who was foreman at the HT ranch not far from where this happened and who later ranched just up Sand Creek from us was in Medora at the time and heard the man tell the story. The men were buried in shallow graves right where they fell. Only one is still marked with a little pile of stones

I talked to my brother Wilmer and he decided to come in on the deal as a partner and Dad said he would help stock it. So with the trade-in of the truck and trailer and a little borrowed money, I was able to make my half of the down payment. Wilmer had no trouble getting his half and so on New Year's Eve 1949 the Elmer Mack Ranch became the Aus Brothers' Ranch. We thought we would surely make our fortunes in the ranching business. But first we had to pay off the ranch and we found out that was easier said than done.

To stock the place the first year, we bought a band of sheep, ran some pasture cattle for Gilman Peterson of South Heart, ran 20 head of mares on shares from Bill Habetzel of Mandan and Dad bought some steers. Eventually we owned enough stock of our own.

The place didn't have very good improvements. The house was a little 3 room affair. The bedroom was too cold to sleep in during the winter, but it was good enough for a couple of bachelors. Our furniture was bare minimum. We had electricity, but no telephone and our running water was made possible by working a pump handle. Later when Wilmer and Grace got married, they moved in a larger house and I moved into the bunk house. Grace was such a good cook that I made a deal to eat with them.

The ranching business is always dependent on the weather. We need rain in the summer and the winter can't be too severe. We don't want hail or too much hot wind.

The first two years after we bought the ranch the weather was favorable. But in the fall of 1951 the weather turned bad in late October. From then on it kept on snowing and blowing, and didn't let up until March. I think it was the longest winter I can remember. We were snowed in for weeks at a time.

Fortunately we had some feed stacked here and there and could ride horse back and pitch it over the fence wherever the stock happened to be. We also fed a lot of cake. We had to pack it out with a pack horse. Most years we didn't feed much besides cake but this year we fed about all the hay we had. The creeks ran high that spring.

There were some beaver on Sand Creek where we lived. They were a real nuisance. They would cut down trees and dam up the creek so it would shut the water off. We would get a permit from the Game & Fish Department to trap some of them but they wouldn't let us take them all so there was always some left for seed. We had to have them tagged by the Game & Fish Department before we could sell the pelts, so they always knew how many beaver we killed. Wilmer was a better trapper than me so he did most of the trapping. I went to check the traps one morning and found a skunk had wandered into one of the traps. Thinking I wouldn't waste a bullet, I picked up a piece of a tree branch about 10 ft. long and I planned to tap him on the head to knock him out and then push him in the water to drown him. That plan didn't work well at all. The skunk was facing me when I hit him, so I thought I was safe. But some how he sprayed over his back and got me right in the face. I found out immediately what a dumb thing it was to do. My eyes stung so bad I took off my cap and stuck my head in the creek. After my eyes cleared a little and I could see again, I took off my jacket and chaps and hung them in a tree and rode home. It was cold riding home without a coat, but I only had a little over a mile to go. I could smell skunk for a week. The skunk ended up dead. We trapped other fur-bearing animals in a small way.

A few years earlier I had a few traps out mostly for coyotes. Dad and I were hauling coal late in the fall and hauling it home with a team and wagon (we had our own coal mine for our own use.) Dad drove the team and I rode horseback so I could check my traps after we got the coal loaded. I had one set made on a ridge above Sand Creek. One morning as I got to within about a quarter of a mile from the set I noticed my horse started to act nervous and the closer I got the more nervous he became. When I got close enough to see what the problem was, he refused to go any nearer. I had caught what I thought was a bobcat. Later Dad told me it was actually a Canadian Lynx. It had the tuft of hair on the tips of its ears and it was much bigger than a bobcat. I had never seen either one before. I killed the cat and thought I'd tie it behind my saddle. I was riding Jigs that day and he would have no part of that. I got the cat home by tying it to the end of my lariat rope and dragging it home.

I rode Jigs for many years after that but for the rest of his life he refused to go near the spot where I caught the cat. Horses and cats are natural enemies. When I got home I lifted it up by its hind legs as high as I could and his front legs touched the ground.

Wilmer and I worked well together most of the time. If we had a disagreement about how things should be done, I usually was stubborn enough to win the argument. Unfortunately it would often turn out that he was right and I was wrong. It was several years before I realized how often that was the case and by that time we were no longer partners as I had moved to Montana. As the saying goes, we are too soon old and too late smart.

I really enjoyed having the ranch. I was young then and it was hard work but I didn't mind the challenge. We had very little equipment when we started out. We didn't even have a pickup. Jeeps were not very common yet so we used horses a lot more than people do now. If we needed to check the livestock or fences or water, we would ride horseback. Our horses were used to working and would do anything we asked of them. We also used them for recreation. Many times on Sunday afternoon my friend Curt would ride over and we would find somewhere to ride and something to do. Sometimes other fellows in the community would show up and we would go catch a wild horse or go to the pasture and rope some cows and ride them with a loose rope around their girth. Later on I started to rodeo and then we didn't do so much foolishness.

Chapter 10

The Badlands Boot & Saddle Club

When Wilmer and I bought the Mack ranch at Amidon, we decided to organize a Saddle Club. There were several young people in the area who liked to do things on horseback besides just the usual ranch work. I put a notice in the local paper and word spread that there would be a meeting at our place west of Amidon. The purpose of the club was to have fun on horseback. We had a good turnout for that first meeting and we organized a club. It was pretty informal, about evenly divided between men and ladies. I was elected the first president.

We learned to do quadrilles and put on performances at several nearby towns. Julius Homelvig was the instructor and caller. We had as many as 24 quadrille riders.

Other saddle clubs got organized around the country so we would compete in games on horseback. We used our imagination to think up games such as scoop shovel races, saddle up races, walk-trot-and run races, ring spearing, Bull Durham races, and so many others I can't remember. Some towns we competed with were New England, Regent, Hettinger, and Lemon, South Dakota.

The bull Durham race was one I thought up myself. I could roll a cigarette pretty fast those days so I thought maybe I would have a chance to win. The game went something like this: A sack of tobacco and papers and 2 wooden matches (we called them farmers' sticks) were placed in a row, one for each contestant. The riders lined up about 100 yards or so from the tobacco. When the starter said go, everyone rode down to his sack of tobacco and rolled a smoke which had to be lit with one of the 2 matches and ride back across the starting line with the cigarette still lit. First one back was the winner.

I smoked a little then. It was the sign of being a big boy. Cowboys were expected to have a sack of tobacco in his shirt pocket with the little tab hanging out. As I remember, there were 3 brands of dry tobacco in little cloth bags -- Bull Durham, Dukes Mixture, and Golden Grain, and they were all a nickel a bag. Ready made cigarettes were Camels, Lucky Strike and Chesterfield. They sold for 20 cents a pack. Later on they made a longer cigarette (King Size) called Pall Mall and then a menthol flavored one called Kools. There was pipe tobacco in tin cans—Velvet, Prince Albert, and Sir Walter Raleigh were the three I remember.

I was never a heavy smoker. I don't think I ever smoked much more than 1/2 dozen smokes a day so one Saturday night I decided as long as I wasn't very good at it I would just give up and quit all together. I laid my makins (tobacco and papers) on my dresser and didn't touch them for 30 days and then threw them away. I never smoked again except for a scene in Old Four Eyes. In one bar room scene Dr. Walsh wanted someone to roll a smoke for effect. So every night I would roll a smoke and light it. But as President Bill Clinton would say, "I never inhaled." No one talked about smoking as being bad for your health those days, but I felt better and now I'm certainly glad I quit early on.

The following story appeared in *Bar North* (a North Dakota magazine) in 1954 written by Mrs. Gilman Peterson.

The Badlands Boot and Saddle Club
By Mrs. Gilman Peterson

When the spectators eagerly crowd the fence around the parade ground or arena, step right

The Badlands Boot and Saddle Club at Amidon

up so you won't miss a minute of the action. It is the Badlands Boot and Saddle Club grand entry. Flag bearers are first in line and all the horses are cantering in rhythm to the music from the huge loud speaker mounted on the truck near the grand stand.

There they line up for your inspection, thirty five cowboys and cowgirls in colorful regalia, and some really beautiful horses. The music changes for the quadrille, each horse and rider responds perfectly as they circle right or left, keeping perfect time to the music and calls from the loud speaker. Interspersed with the quadrilles are various horse races and novelty races until, with the grand finale the members have presented a complete horse show, to the immense enjoyment of everyone present.

The Badlands Boot and Saddle Club was organized in 1951. There were thirty five

The Badlands Boot and Saddle Club on parade.

members the first year, with the membership growing each year since.

Merle Aus was elected the first president.

Home territory for the club is the Aus brothers ranch a few miles west of Amidon on the edge of the Little Missouri badlands.

We kept the Saddle Club going for a few years. We called it the Badlands Boot and Saddle Club. Eventually the enthusiasm started to slip. Max Wilson and I started to go to rodeos on weekends and so the Saddle Cub just faded away. It was fun while it lasted. About the last thing the club did was to build a rodeo arena and put on a rodeo in Amidon.

Chapter 11

Rodeoing

I heard lots of stories about rodeos in the early days before my time. Amidon had its share of good hands. I was told Elmer Clark, who grew up in the badlands north of Amidon was the first one to ride the famous bucking horse Tiperary. This happened at a rodeo at Buffalo, S.D. some time in the 1920s. I knew Elmer when he was our county commissioner in Slope county. I would try to see Elmer when he would come to meetings in Amidon because he was such a funny guy and great story teller. He and his wife had a son they called Merle. He rodeoed too and when I would see him he would say I was the guy with the funny name. The Clarks ranched on the Little Missouri River.

Then there were the well known Davis brothers. They grew up just north of Amidon and all were good hands. They all had nicknames. There was Schoony, Speck, Pussy, Pistol, Jack and Floyd. I knew them all except Pussy, but I wasn't old enough to see them ride. They had quit before I knew them. They also had a sister, Wilma. She married Gordon Alexander and was our neighbor. They had 3 girls, Betty, Ruth and Marie, and a boy Russ. Russ was a good friend and ran the home place after Gordon died. Marie married Curt Homelvig and Betty married Stan Holzmer. Ruth went east to school and stayed.

Not many rodeos survived the depression and then the war. But after the war nearly all county fairs in the western part of North Dakota built arenas and put on rodeos. Some with the most population put on professional PRCA rodeos. That meant only contestants who belonged to the Professional Rodeo Cowboys Association could compete. Smaller towns put on amateur rodeos because it didn't cost as much. At these rodeos any ranch cowboys could compete and the competition wasn't so tough and the entry fees were usually less. The organization of cowboys wasn't always called the PRCA. It started out as the Turtles in the 1930s and 40s then it became the Rodeo Cowboys Association until sometime in the 1980s when it became the Professional Rodeo Cowboy Association, (PRCA.)

A lot of outstanding rodeo cowboys grew up in North Dakota. During the 1950s and 60s six P.R.C.A. cowboys that traveled together were affectionately called the six pack. They were all outstanding rough stock riders and all champions. They all went back to ranching when they retired from rodeoing. (Their names were- Tescher brothers, Jim and Tom, Alvin Nelson, Dean Armstrong, Joe Chase, and Duane Howard.) The six pack was by no means the only good rodeo hands that came from North Dakota. Many more made it to the National Finals Rodeo. I'm proud to say I knew most of them except the younger ones who have become famous the last few years.

Montana has also produced many famous rodeo hands. I am not as well acquainted with the Montana hands because I did more rodeoing in North Dakota. Many good cowboys had talent enough to reach the top in the standings but did not choose to travel as much as was necessary to achieve the top ranking. There are also good ranch cowboys who do not wish to exhibit their talents at all but make good use of their abilities on the ranch.

I do not agree with writers who say the day of the cowboy is over. The dictionary describes a cowboy as one who makes a living on a horse. It does not say one has to ride all day every day. Cowboys now have to be more versatile than the cowboys of long ago. I think there are many good cowboys today and also a few wanna-bes.

Bowman County built a new arena at the fair grounds in Bowman sometime in the late 1940's and scheduled an amateur rodeo. I was having a little work done on my truck that day and the bill came to $5. The entry fee for the cow riding was $5 and all I had in my wallet was $5. My friends Bud Mack, Clark Spethman, Lee Hestigan, and Don Hill were entering and I sure wanted to, too. I took a chance and entered my first rodeo. I drew a good cow and got her rode. I didn't win but I placed and got a check for $35. That was quite a bit of money in those days and I thought if I kept going to rodeos I'd never have another poor day. Well, I kept going to rodeos but I had some poor days.

Cow riding and steer riding was an amateur event. Eventually Jim Barnhart got some Brahma steers. They put on a little better show and were a little harder to ride but they didn't get mean or on the fight like bulls sometimes do.

Then John Stevenson, a stock contractor from Carson, North Dakota, who also produced amateur rodeos got a string of Brahma bulls. The first time I entered the bull riding, I lay awake all night wondering if I would survive. I drew a big gray bull with a big hump. He was a fresh bull that nobody knew. I was really nervous until my bull came in the chute. When I got busy getting my bull rope on him and getting down on him I calmed down a bit.

I actually enjoyed the ride. He jumped high but went straight and when the whistle blew, I was surprised to still be on the bull. I was close to the fence when I jumped off. As soon as I did, he turned and came to eat me. I tried to get under the fence but he stepped on my leg. There was no clown, but Alfred Lorenz ran out waving a saddle blanket so the bull forgot about me. My leg got a little black and blue but I survived my first bull ride. I didn't win the bull riding, but I placed so I was encouraged to go again. However I was getting to the age when a more mature mind said it was time to pursue other events. I was glad team roping was becoming an event at most rodeos because older men and women could still be a part of rodeos.

Another event I liked to enter was the wild cow milking. I was lucky in getting good hands to mug for me. Some that I remember were, Tiny Engesser, Chuck Hawkinson, Billy Olson and Jim Cook. At most rodeos the wild cow milking was what we called a mad scramble where a bunch of cows were put at one end of the arena and the cowboys were lined up at the other end all mounted and ready to rope. When the whistle blew, all the cowboys rode down to rope a cow. The muggers would then get hold of the cow's head and hold them while the ropers got a squirt of milk in a bottle and ran back to the judge. Obviously the first one back with some milk was the winner.

I had a strategy. When the whistle blew, instead of trying to be the first one to get to the cows, I would hold back a little and when the other ropers got to the bunch, the cows would scatter and then I would take after the first cow to start up along the fence. I'd chase it back toward the judge before I'd rope it so I wouldn't have so far to run with the milk. Sometimes it worked. One time I remember getting my cow caught really fast and she was a nice cow so my mugger got her stopped quick and I was the first one to get some milk in my bottle. I started to run back to the judge thinking I had plenty of time when all of a sudden I heard someone coming behind me. It was Vern Anderson and he had enough momentum to go by me like a bullet. He beat me to the judge so I had to take 2nd. That was another case of "If I'da", an excuse so often heard around rodeos. If I'da just run faster.

Team tying, later team roping, was my favorite event. In team tying, one member of the team ropes the horns or the head and the other member, who is called the heeler, ropes the heels and stretches the cow out. Then the header gets off and tails the steer down and ties a short rope around the steer's back legs below the hocks and above the dew claws with a square knot. This was changed later on to team roping which is not so time consuming. In this event the header ropes the horns and the heeler ropes the hind feet. The ropes are pulled tight and the horses face each other and that's all there is to it. It goes much faster than team tying.

When I first started rodeoing, there was no team roping but soon Jim Barnhart, who was producing amateur rodeos, started to have it at his rodeos. None of us had ever done this before so it was sure enough an amateur event.

The first time I entered the team tying was at Belfield, North Dakota, I think it was about 1955. I didn't have a partner but as I pulled in to the rodeo grounds a tall lean fellow pulled up beside me. We didn't know each other then but we got acquainted and decided we'd rope together. That was Rex Cook and we got to be good friends. This was team tying and most of the ropers had not even seen this done. I had been to the famous La Fiesta De Los Vaqueros rodeo in Tucson, Arizona, and watched the team tying. There was a lot of missing at Belfield that day. Finally a team made a run and I heard someone say, "No one will beat that." But we hadn't gone yet and we got it done 10 seconds faster. Our time wouldn't win much these days but we got lucky and came up with the win. I'll say again: I'd rather be lucky than good. I've also said to win at team roping you need a good horse, a good partner and lots of luck. Good luck, that is. I've had both kinds. I've had streaks of good luck and streaks of bad luck. I'd rather talk about the good luck.

It was about 1956 when I ran into Rex one day in Dickinson. He told me that George Wolf, the saddle maker at the Western Trading Post had quit and Andrew Johnston, the owner, was looking for a hand to replace him. He suggested that I go apply for the job. Rex was a good saddle maker and had just taught me the basics of doing leather work such as tooling belts and billfolds and doing some saddle repair and he was confident I would get along all-right in the shop. So I went to talk to Andrew. He had owned the shop since he retired from ranching several years before. I found him in his shop hand stitching some leather and I noticed the way his hands shook that he was having a hard time sewing in a straight line. I explained to him that I was a beginner and that Rex had helped me get started. Rex had worked for Andrew sometime previous. I didn't want to work full time so that I could help at the ranch part of the time. I agreed to work four days a week from 7 A. M. to 5 P.M. for $8 a day. I didn't accumulate a big fortune but I gained a lot of experience.

Andrew had a pretty good knowledge of repairing saddles which turned out to be the bulk of the work I did there. With Rex living right there in Dickinson I could get advice any time I needed it.

I enjoyed working there and I was learning every day. Cowboys and ranchers would come in to get saddles and tack repaired or to have items made or to just kill time. I never got bored. Andrew had some stories to tell too as he had come to the country before 1900. I did quite a bit of work for Native Americans. They liked fancy belts and other items to wear at pow wows. I was unfamiliar with that sort of thing but they would explain what they wanted and I could usually make it for them. I admire the way they stick to their culture.

In 1958 Walt Schaaf put on a roping at his place in Belfield. It was restricted to North Dakota ropers. Rex and I entered together. This was still team tying. It was a three go around roping and the winner was to be declared the North Dakota Champions. We won the first go around with 19 sec. The second go we caught but took too long to place. After two rounds we were behind Tex Appledorn and Tom Olson by 5/10 seconds. Most other teams had missed at least one steer. We tied our third steer in 25 so Tex and

Tom had a good chance to beat us. But we were lucky again. When Tex caught their steer and turned back, a horn broke and the steer got away. That happens very rarely but it let us become the North Dakota State Champion Team Tiers. We each got a nice silver belt buckle. Not many rodeos or ropings those days had buckles to give away. Yet some of the best and luckiest guys accumulate a lot of them over a lifetime. I have won only 5 but I feel lucky to have those.

I roped with Jim Botch from Wibaux one summer. (This was after we moved to Montana.) We went to quite a few rodeos, most all the ones close by. We never won 1st at any of them but as I remember we placed at all of them except at Terry, Montana, where somehow Jim's rope got under his horse's tail and the horse started bucking. Jim got up a little dusty but not hurt so we all had a good laugh. Jim was a good sport and he had to laugh, too. I think that was the last year we did team tying. We started team roping the next year. There was beginning to be a lot or ropers and team roping was less time consuming, plus it was less stress on the steers.

My good friend Ralph Nelson and I roped together one summer. We picked up a check or two but we were both better heelers than headers so he started roping with Ray Granmoe and I went with Gene (Pete) Pedersen. We both did better that way.

Pete and I went to a few jack pots the first year we roped together and had pretty good luck. Then Tex and Pauline Appledorn put on a century roping at Medora for anyone who lived in North Dakota or had lived and rodeoed in North Dakota. To qualify for the century roping the two partners' ages had to add up to 100 years. I was 50 that year and Pete was a couple years older so we qualified. It was a two steer average and there were buckles for the winners. 57 teams entered.

We won the first go around but Tex Appledorn and Les Best were right on our heels for the average. On the last steer they were up before us, so we knew how fast we had to be to win. I told Pete we couldn't be over 12, but let's be eight. He turned the steer about half way down the arena and I got lucky. We were 10 flat and won the buckles. I was also entered with Bob Erickson and we won third so I had a pretty good day. Times weren't as fast those days as they are now.

The next winter Ron Rocklitz put on a roping at their place west of Wibaux. It was 3 steers a Sunday for 6 Sundays for a total of 18 steers. There wasn't much money in the pot but the winners would each get a trophy saddle. I really wanted to win a saddle. The winner was determined by the most total money won. Beginning the last day Pete and I were $4 in the lead. When it came down to the last steer, all we had to do was catch. As soon as I saw Pete's rope go on the horns, I caught the heels. Then a disappointing thing happened. A horn must have broken and the rope popped off the head. We were allowed three loops those days but we already used up 2 so we got a no time. Had I waited a little while before I heeled the steer, Pete could have rebuilt a loop and caught him again. Then if I didn't miss the heels, we would have gotten a time and won the saddles. According to today's rule I would have been flagged out for cross firing (roping the heels before the header had control of the steer). So we ended up $4 short. Glen Hutchinson and Harold Bakken won the saddles. Ray Granmoe and Sam Selman were 2nd by 10¢ and we were third. That is as close as I have ever come to winning a saddle.

I think it was the summer of 1984 the National Old Timers Rodeo Association was in full swing. There was an age restriction on the contestants. No one under age forty was allowed and each contestant competed in his or her age bracket. There were 3 age brackets, 40 to 50, 50 to 60, and over 60.

This was a nationwide organization and results were recorded just like the PRCA. Pete and I entered in the 60 and over. We made it to Great Falls, Harlowton, Roundup, Forsyth, Glendive, Miles City, and Gillette, WY. At the end of the season if you were in the top 35 in the nation you qualified to compete in the national finals. I think it was held in Amarillo, Texas, but I don't remember for sure. It was the 1st part of November and I was running for county commissioner that year and the election was the same time so I thought I'd better stay home and campaign. I should have gone to the rodeo as I was defeated by the incumbent. That was my first and last attempt at running for political office.

I think the Old Timers Rodeo Association has died. At least I haven't heard of any rodeos for several years, none in this area anyway.

Rodeo has become an intercollegiate sport. Dawson Community College didn't have a rodeo program when Rose Marie first become a member of the faculty but I think it was about 1971 when a group of students wanted to form a rodeo club. They were required to have a faculty member to be their adviser so they asked Rose Marie if she would do that. She agreed to help them and a rodeo club was formed.

Rose Marie was the adviser for a few years and then turned it over to Tom Ree. In 1981 the Dawson boys won the National Intercollegiate Rodeo Association

Championship. Pretty good for the smallest college in the nation with a rodeo team.

Years ago team roping was not a PRCA sanctioned event. I don't remember when some of the rodeos in this area started to sanction the event, probably in the 1970's. Pete had been a member for many years so I bought a permit and we entered our first PRCA rodeo together on the 4th of July in Killdeer, North Dakota. The professional cowboys hadn't had time to practice much yet and they let us win it with 10 sec. flat. Ten wouldn't win much nowadays. Five seconds might place on a cold day.

Then my luck suddenly went the other way. I couldn't seem to do anything right. I made every mistake possible. I went to a jack pot in Miles City one day. I entered with two good partners. It was a three header. One partner caught all three and I missed them all. The other partner missed all three. As the old saying goes, If it wouldn't have been for bad luck, I wouldn't have had any luck at all. That's kind of the way things went for a while. Not that I never picked up another check but my turn didn't come around as often as it used to. C.L. Askins gave me some good advice which helped some but once you go into a slump, your confidence goes down, too. I had a lot of fun rodeoing and roping. I met a lot of fun people and maybe I won my share. I just didn't end up winning at the end. Maybe my age had something to do with it. I stuck with it until I was 74 years old when I had to quit riding entirely. Because of a serious illness I lost my sense of balance. My riding and rodeoing came to an end forever.

I look back now and realize we didn't put much effort into our rodeoing. Nowadays people who rodeo practice every day they are not on the road. I seldom practiced and I thought if I went to a dozen rodeos a year I was really going places. We just didn't have the time to play any more than that. I'm sure our times would have improved had we had the time to practice and gone to some roping schools. Poor excuses are better than none I guess.

I am certainly glad I was able to rodeo even though I didn't go professionally. I met so many good people that I probably would not have met otherwise. To be able to win occasionally was nice but since we were amateurs and not doing it to make a living we were probably more relaxed and competed mostly for the fun of it. Most of us had ranches to run and didn't have a lot of time to devote to rodeos. The friends I made at rodeos over so many years made it all worth while.

Chapter 12

Medora

Early in the spring of 1958 I read in the local paper that there were plans underway for an outdoor theater to be built at Medora and a play about Theodore Roosevelt's life in the North Dakota Badlands would be done that summer. It would be several nights a week all summer until Labor Day. What caught my attention was the fact that there would be ten horses in the show. The article said they were looking for people to be in the show and if anyone was interested there would be a meeting scheduled in Medora. I thought that sounded like fun and maybe I could get a job handling the horses. If it turned out to be something big I didn't want to be left out so I went to the meeting. The sponsor of the whole operation was the Theodore Roosevelt National Park and Badlands Association. I think there were about 12 members on the board who were overseers of the Roosevelt Park at Medora and they hired Dr. Fred Walsh to direct the show. Dr. Walsh was the Chairman of the Speech and Drama Department at North Dakota State University in Fargo at the time. Thomas Patterson from North Carolina wrote the play. I knew only two members of the board. One was Jim Barnhart who put on a lot of amateur rodeos around that part of North Dakota. The other was Clara Brown the Superintendent of Schools in Slope County, my home.

When I got to the meeting I was handed a script of the play and Dr. Walsh asked me to read a couple of paragraphs. I had never been in a play even in school so I was taken aback. I only had in mind to take care of the horses and maybe doing something backstage. I'm not a good reader, especially if I can't see it ahead of time. I tried to explain that I was experienced with horses and I could even bring some horses and saddles of my own. But he didn't seem to pay much attention to that so I didn't think I had much of a chance to be a part of the show.

I was surprised a couple of weeks later when I received a contract in the mail. It said I was to report for work June 1st and I was to play the part of Joe Ferris. Joe Ferris was a store owner in Medora and also a hunting guide. Roosevelt came to Medora to shoot a buffalo.

According to Theodore Roosevelt's account of his life in the Badlands, Joe Ferris was his guide when he killed a buffalo (the last one killed in that area).

The play was written to follow the facts quite accurately according to Herman Hagedorn, expert on the life of Teddy Roosevelt.

So I reported to Medora on the 1st day of June1958. We went out to the site where the theater was to be built. Some dirt work had been done on a steep hillside. A little flat spot had been leveled for a stage and the hillside was smoothed off to be the seating. It was a perfect natural amphitheater. There was a big pile of rough lumber and another one of scoria, which is a red shale often used on roads. It is found on many of the hills in the area. Our job was to build a theater, learn our lines, get the horses used to the stage, make costumes, rehearse the show and be ready by the 29th of June. Out of the 29 days, we rained out ten days. We were running out of time to get the theater ready. On rainy days we found an empty building down town and rehearsed our lines.

The first day at work I looked around to see what our work crew looked like. Everyone in the show was expected to work, either in construction, or costumes, or publicity. Most of the actors were young drama students from eastern colleges, such as Hofstra and Boston College. Most of them wore shorts which at that time in the little cow town of Medora was neither seen nor approved of. By the color of their skin it was obvious to me they hadn't had much exposure to sunshine. That was the construction crew.

The first thing to do was to dig holes to put in supports for the bleachers. I noticed three or four guys in a group with a posthole digger looking pretty confused, so I went over and asked if I could help. They looked relieved and admitted they were having trouble digging a hole. I showed them how to use the digger, a hand digger of course. When they saw how easy it was they all looked amazed and one said to me, "Wow! You must be a real cowboy." By the end of the first day most of the young men had blisters on their hands but were feeling good about what they were learning and what they had accomplished. They were all good boys and willing to work but were from a different environment so had to learn everything as we went along. Three of these fellows helped me with the horses and we got along good. There were a few mistakes now and again but we had gentle horses so there weren't any bad wrecks. One night a bridle was put on backwards so the curb strap was riding over the horses' nose but I happened to notice it before we left the corral.

Bill Strange was a high school teacher from Wibaux. Bill knew how to work and understood electronics so he was put in charge of installing the lighting for the stage. Bill Lawson was an older fellow who lived his whole life around Medora. He had a little problem with alcohol. He just had a small part in the show playing a gambler. I heard that latter on, he was taken in by a kindly doctor in Beach, North Dakota, stopped drinking and become the doctor's handyman. I got along good with Bill so I was glad he got sobered up.

Bob Jones was a rancher and banker in Beach and Hollis Dietz was a highway patrolman. They were very helpful in keeping us supplied with building material and also in an advisory capacity. Also helping with the construction were Father Fahnlander's boys from Home on the Range, a home for troubled boys in Sentinel Butte N. D. They were fun to have around, (so full of energy and willing to do anything asked of them.)

Bucky Nunn was the young grandson of Jim Barnhart. I think he was 12 years old at the time. Jim had a bunch of bucking horses and Bucky was spending the summer herding them for his granddad. Bucky's part in the show was to ride up a ridge with some other vigilantes who had captured a horse thief and when they came to a suitable tree he was to throw the hangman's noose over a high limb so they could hang the rascal. Bucky was a good little horse hand and he practiced throwing the rope over the limb and never missed until the night his parents came to see him perform. His second try was successful and the horse thief got what he deserved.

There had to be a lot done to get publicity out, especially the first year. One day several of us dressed like bandits and when the Greyhound bus came into town we rode our horses out in front of it with guns drawn. When the driver stopped we ordered everyone to get out of the bus and to stand in a group. Then Dr. Walsh stepped forward and explained that it was just a publicity stunt and apologized for the inconvenience. We got the name and address of everyone and the name, of course, of their local newspaper. There was a cameraman there and pictures were sent to the newspapers explaining about the upcoming performances. That spread the word far and wide. The bus was full of people from all over the country. It might be a little dangerous to try a stunt like that nowadays with so many people carrying weapons.

A few days after the show opened the TV show "Queen for a Day" sent their queen to Medora. I don't remember much about "Queen for a Day" except that it was a weekly show on one of the networks. Some women were interviewed and the one whom they thought most deserving would be declared queen for a day and they would send her to some interesting place where she would be entertained. Medora has always been a place of historic interest because of Teddy Roosevelt and the Marquis de Mores. Now with the theater it became more of a tourist town.

To show the Queen a real western welcome a few of us were asked to be on the street horseback when she arrived. She was chauffeured into town in a fancy convertible. A small local country western band was playing in the street. After the introductions to the town folks I was to ask her if she would like to dance.

I was honored but also a little apprehensive. Would she turn me down and could she dance our style? I finally built up enough courage to get off my horse and go ask her. She said she would be delighted so I asked the band to play a waltz and we danced out in the street. I was wearing chaps and spurs,(not good for dancing.) She was a good dancer and a very nice lady. We had a nice visit, and she was very complementary about the hospitality of the North Dakota folks and thought Medora was a pretty neat town. She was shown the town and the Theodore Roosevelt Park and the Chateau De Mores. That night they brought her to the show. She said she had a really good time. The next day she went back to her home in California with pleasant memories of Medora, North Dakota.

Because 1958 was the 100 year anniversary of Teddy Roosevelt's birth the National Geographic sent a young man out to Medora to do a story. His name was Thomas Abercrombie and I got to show him around. We rode horse back in the badlands a couple of days so he could take pictures and went to the Maltese Cross Ranch where Joe Hild was branding calves. This was Teddy's first ranch when he came to North Dakota. Tom had never ridden a horse before and he told me he thought he would hate riding and was afraid the local cowboys would make fun of him. That didn't happen. In fact he took to horseback riding like a duck to water. It wasn't long before I had trouble keeping him from running his horse too hard. He was on the staff of National Geographic for many years and wrote stories about strange places all over the globe and he was fun to have around. Even though we were in a race against time to get the show ready and the theater finished by the 29th of June Dr. Walsh sent me out with Abercrombie because I knew the badlands and I knew the horses and he said it was good for publicity. I was lucky again.

The theater was built in a natural amphitheater where the seating for 1500 people was built on a steep side hill and the stage was flattened out at the bottom. The center stage was part of the town of Medora. The right stage was Roosevelt's cabin on the Maltese cross and on the left side we did some range scenes like branding a calf. This was all built out of rough lumber and slabs. The idea was to make things look as rustic as possible. We had a pretty sophisticated lighting system but the acoustics were so good in that setting we didn't need any amplification. While the audience was waiting for the show to start they looked out over the Little Missouri River and the badlands. What a pretty sight that was.

On the 29th of June things were getting tense. We were fairly confident that we knew our parts but we still had work to do on the set. I had the horses pretty well lined out. I didn't have quite enough horses of my own so we rented some from Jim Barnhart and Walt Ray and a team from Pete Northrop. The horses were all good dependable horses and the team I used to take Teddy hunting was black, well matched and really drove nice.

We finally finished building the set a few minutes before 7 p.m. when the people were allowed to come down to find their seats for the 8 p.m. performance. Dr. Walsh was very strict about any of the cast members being seen by the audience before the show started. We had to stay in the dressing room out of sight.

We got the show started on time. Teddy (played by Dave Lohman from Maddock, North Dakota) killed a buffalo, the horse thief was hanged, the boat thieves were captured and Teddy and the Marquis De'Mores almost fought a duel. We thought everything went pretty smooth. Dr. Walsh and J. B. Flesner, the stage manager, seemed quite pleased. J.B. was an older man who had spent his entire life in show business and it was good to have someone with experience to be the stage manager. He also played the Marquis, a French nobleman who came to Medora about the same time Teddy did. His big plan was to build a packing plant in Medora and ship the meat in refrigerated railroad cars to the east coast. The smoke stack for the packing plant is still standing in Medora and is a historic sight. The plan was a failure but the Marquis became well known. His wife's name was Medora and he named the town Medora in her honor.

Although the play went well that first night our good luck lasted quick. Shortly after the performance was over and we got the props put away there was a flash of lightning and a big clap of thunder, the sky opened up and we had a cloudburst. We had to take the horses about a half a mile to where we kept them

The theater we built in the badlands near Medora.

at night. It was pretty scary riding in all that lightning and of course we got soaking wet.

Early the next morning we got a call to come to work. There was a lot of damage to the theater. The scoria on the long winding path from the top of the hill to the stage below and also between the bleachers had mostly all washed down onto the stage. Everyone went to work and we were again ready to go, we lost only one night's performance. J.B. said it was just one of the challenges of show business. He said there was only 2 things you had to give an actor time to do. You have to allow time to eat and time to go to church if they wanted to. Sleep is something you do when you get a chance.

The play was called 'Old Four Eyes' after the nickname the local cowboys called Teddy Roosevelt. No one in the area wore glasses those days except Roosevelt so they called him Four Eyes. The theater had seating for 1500 people and Dr. Walsh wouldn't allow more than 1500 tickets to be sold each night There were always more people that came to see the show than could get tickets so they were turned away. On the 4th of July that first year we turned away 400 car loads of people. We thought the show was a success. That first year there were cars from every state but 4 to see the 33 performances ending on Labor Day.

Because the show was so successful the first year the 1959 season was expanded to 50 performances, several more staff members were hired and a gift shop was added. I furnished most of the horses and my salary was increased favorably. It was going to be a good summer. I didn't realize at first just how good it was going to be. Among the new people hired that year was a young lady who had just finished her first year of teaching high school English at Hallock,

Minnesota. She hadn't reported for work yet on the second day and Dr. Walsh was getting concerned. The next day we were working on the set when we heard a car coming. It was Rose Marie Goetz driving a 1948 Chevy. She was chugging along followed by a cloud of blue smoke. She had been having car trouble coming from Minnesota and the car wouldn't make the steep hill to the parking lot that was for the cast and staff. The Chevy needed help. Several of the guys ran down to help the damsel in distress but I kept on doing what I was doing.

That night there was a small party of cast members and I noticed Rose Marie was there. We got acquainted and 13 days later we decided to get married. We would have to wait a year to get married because Rose Marie had already signed a contract to teach another year at Hallock, Minnesota, and people didn't break contracts in those days.

It was the most exiting summer of my life. Rose Marie and I spent every spare minute together. We put on 5 performances a week and usually every night after the show and after we took care of the horses the whole cast would gather in some coulie where we would sing songs and tell stories till daylight. Dave Lommen, (Teddy Roosevelt in the show), could sing cowboy songs in the German language. That was really entertaining. I guess we averaged 3 hours of sleep a night. But it was fun.

I was renting horseback rides to dudes in the daytime and sometimes they would want to go early in the morning so there wasn't much time for sleep. Some days I didn't have any customers so then Rose Marie and I would just hang out.

The second year the foundation brought in a bunch of used trailer houses for the cast members to sleep in instead of renting rooms all over town. They were parked by a vacant ranch house a couple miles from the theater. They also hired a cook to feed us. The food was great and we enjoyed the camaraderie.

After doing the same show night after night, it was easy to let your mind wander about other things besides doing the best job of acting, maybe even forgetting a line or just not putting enough energy into it. When that happened, Dr. Walsh would always notice and he would call a rehearsal. Usually that would be immediately after the performance. On those nights the partying got a late start. Sometimes the gathering would be at the Log Cabin Bar downtown. It was a rustic little place and the bartender was Gaylord Barnhart. He played a honky-tonk piano and sang clever little songs that he must have written, at least I had never heard them before. Gaylord was Jim Barnhart's son. Jim and his wife Hattie owned the bar and a grocery store next door. Jim was very good to everyone in the show.

Jim used to promote Medora as a historic town because Theodore Roosevelt and the Marquis de Mores lived there. Also the badlands are very pretty and scenic. It was a favorite place for trail rides and vacations for people who lived further east and wanted to get away from the hustle and bustle. Otherwise the town of Medora was a quiet little cow town where the area ranch folk could get some groceries and perhaps their mail, but no place to buy a shirt or a new pair of boots. The courthouse for Billings County was at Medora so folks could pay their taxes there. The entrance to the Roosevelt National Park was at Medora so that brought a little traffic to town.

The first year of the show I stayed in the Rough Riders Hotel during the month of June when we had to be at work every day building the theater and re-hearsal at night. After that I drove back and forth to the ranch because we showed only 3 nights a week. Subsequent years we showed 5 nights a week and then with renting horses in the daytime I didn't have time to drive home. Wilmer took good care of the ranch.

The Rough Riders Hotel was a historical landmark. Teddy Roosevelt kept a room there for when he came in from one of his ranches. It was left pretty much the same as when Teddy stayed there. The rooms were all on the second floor. They were tiny and bare with only a bed and a small dresser. No closet, just a few pegs on the wall to hang your clothes. There was a bathroom but it was down the hall. The water pres-sure was intermittent and weak at best. But it was a place to rest in case we got a chance. The hotel has been completely rebuilt now and it is really nice. The rustic appearance has been retained.

Jim Barnhart was the big promoter of Medora. He would see that things happened occasionally. Twice a year he would put on amateur rodeos and Saturday night dances. The local ranchers would all be there. Most of them were young those days. It was fun. After Rose Marie came on the scene, it didn't matter much whether there was anything going on or not just so we could be together, and we were every minute we weren't working. This was the summer of 1959.

It was impossible to travel very far to rodeos during the time I was involved in Old Four Eyes be-cause I had to be back so early in the evening, but I did get to a few close by. Some times some of the cast would go watch and the announcer would introduce us and we would have to stand up. I made sure that none of the actors was wearing shorts to the rodeo because that was a no-no in cowboy land those days.

I would have been embarrassed. Long hair was also considered in bad taste. It's pretty common nowadays. Dean Copping was a top steer wrestler and he wore a full beard for a while, but he was the only one I can remember. I was told he shaved it off because little kids were afraid of him but I don't know that for sure. Dean was well known in eastern Montana and western North Dakota because of the help he gave to so many young fellows starting out in steer wrestling (or bull dogging as some call it.) Dean was well known and well liked so people accepted him with his beard. Nowadays men wear all sorts of different styles of beards and long hair, so no one pays much attention to it.

It was hard to leave Medora that fall. Rose Marie left for Hallock, Minnesota, to her teaching job at the high school there. It wasn't many weeks before I made a trip to Hallock, which is in the extreme northwestern corner of Minnesota. It's a little farming community of Norwegians in the Red River Valley. In fact, we were able to get together several times that fall. Once I delivered a colt to Fargo for Barb Secrest. She and her husband Tom were living in Fargo and Barb had gotten a colt from the Rabes at the HT ranch just west of our ranch near Amidon. Barb and Nancy Rabe were good friends and so was I. Rose Marie drove down to Fargo in her brand new Volkswagen beetle that cost $1775.

Another weekend that fall there was a rodeo in Minot, North Dakota. so Rose Marie came on the train and I took her back to Hallock on Sunday after the rodeo. We stayed in Minot with Dave and Jan Lomman, who were teaching there. Dave had played the part of Teddy Roosevelt in "Old Four Eyes" and Jan also had a part in the show.

Chapter 13

I Went South

After spending Thanksgiving with the Goetz family in Harvey, North Dakota, I left for Arizona to spend a little time on the desert. Again I left the ranch for Wilmer to take care of, knowing it was in good hands.

I had gotten a new 1959 GMC pickup the spring before and I built a miniature saddle shop on the back. I took a few leather tools with me, so I could stop at riding stables and ranches and fix saddles.

Tom Olson and family had bought a ranch near Duncan, Arizona, so I headed that way when I first got to the south land. When I got there I found Gary and Cliff Obrigewitch from the Belfield, North Dakota, area. I knew them from rodeos. They were bronc riders as were several of their cousins. I was glad to see them. They had rented a little cabin in Mesa and I threw my bedroll in with them. We worked in a sale barn in Phoenix a couple days a week and other days I went looking for saddles to fix.

One day it was cold and rainy out and the boys went with me to look for leather work. We stopped at a riding stable where they had close to 100 saddles. Some of them needed work so we started in. The head wrangler didn't have any customers that day because of the weather. He had a little fire built near the tack shed to keep warm and had a big coffee pot full of water on to boil. When it was time to put the coffee in, he didn't use a measure but dumped in 3 or 4 big handfuls of grounds. Then he let it boil for quite some time. When he thought it was done, he poured each of us a tin cup of the brew. You can imagine what it was like. When it had cooled a little, we each took a sip and looked at each other wondering what to do with it. Cliff managed to drink about half of his, but Gary and I waited until the wrangler was temporarily gone and we dumped it in the fire. When the wrangler came back, I guess he caught on that we didn't like his coffee. He said when he goes to the mountains camping he makes his coffee strong then you only need one cup. He had that right.

There were 3 livestock sales rings in the Phoenix area. One sold several used saddles each week. Those that needed repairs usually sold fairly reasonable so I bought one or two each week and repaired them and resold them the next week.

The ranch Tom Olson bought was in the mountains and was owned by Babe and Pearl Waddel. Tom and his family were in the process of moving and the Waddels were still living in the house. We stayed with them a few days and I rebuilt a saddle for Babe while we were there.

The Waddels were really nice people, fun to be around and we got to be good friends right away. Babe was a real cowboy and a great story teller. He stood about 6 foot 6 or better and Pearl was barely 5. It got fairly cold there at night so we would sit around the fire place and play dominoes. They were at retirement age, but they planned to move to a smaller place further up the mountain. A few years later Rose Marie and I took our first trip to Arizona together and spent a couple days with them at the new location. This was in the summer and Babe was having trouble with screw worms in his herd of Santa Gertrudis cattle.

I rode with him one day and helped doctor some calves. He had some good Appaloosa saddle horses. They were well broke. They got rode every day during fly season. Ranchers in the south used to have a problem with screw worms during the hot summers. A certain species of fly would lay eggs in any fresh wound or most often in the navel of new born calves. These eggs when hatched would become screw worms or maggots and if not treated would eventually kill the animal. This is not such a big problem in the northern states because these flies seem to prefer hotter climates although it can happen. I've seen it more with sheep. It is not such a problem in the south now. A system has been devised where the flies are raised in captivity. They are sterilized by radiation and released. The sterilized flies mate with flies in the wild so the fly population is pretty much controlled. That is one government program that works.

When Rose Marie and I left Waddels, we were headed for Nogales to spend a little time in Old Mexico. We were processed at the border by a middle aged Mexican gentleman at a typewriter. As he typed each name, he would read aloud the names of each person. He would have trouble pronouncing some of the gringo names, but when he came to Rose Marie, he brightened up and said in a loud voice, "Rosa Maria." I turned around so he wouldn't see me grinning and there stood the Waddels and Pearl's sister and her husband. They decided to come and spend the day with us. We were happy to see them and we had a good time. They knew their way around the city. People who live within driving distance of the border often go there to shop because things are cheaper there, especially prescription drugs.

Merchants in Mexico like to dicker on price. Often you can buy things for half the price offered at first. Jewelry, pottery and horse tack are for sale in large quantity at reasonable prices but sometimes the quality isn't the best.

This wasn't the first time I had been to Arizona. The first time was the winter of 1956. I was still single but Wilmer was married and had his family started. We talked it over and decided we both didn't need to stay home all winter so I could slip away for a while. So the first part of January I threw my saddle and suitcase in my '49 Chevy car, which had seen its best days, and took off south. I had $200 in my pocket and I expected to find work when I got to Arizona.

I had never seen the Denver Stock Show so I planned the trip down so I could take in a couple days of it. Ernest (Ole) Paska, who used to live near Amidon and whose place is now part of our place, lived in the south of Denver. He invited me to stay with him and his wife while I was there and I accepted. As I was coming into Denver, the brakes went out on my car. This was about 5:00 p.m. and the traffic was scary with or without brakes. Fortunately this old clunker had a manual transmission, so I could use it to slow

down. Needless to say, I didn't break any speed records. I happened to pass an auto parts store so I
stopped and bought a master cylinder kit. When I got
to Oles' place, I crawled under the car and changed
the parts so I had brakes again. I don't claim to be a
master mechanic but cars were much simpler to work
on those days.

I stayed nearly a week in Denver. I had a good time
and went to the stock show and rodeo several times.
By mingling with the cowboys I was able to see the
rodeo without buying a ticket. That helped a lot with
my meager budget. Ole and I had some enjoyable time
together. He had been a good horseman and was a
fun storyteller. We laughed a lot and I learned a lot
about getting along with horses.

When I got ready to leave Denver, I had $90 in my
pocket, but my car was running and I had brakes.
Gas was cheap then. I think it was around 30 cents
a gallon

As I drove south, I kept expecting the weather to
turn warmer, but it didn't. I drove on ice quite a bit
until I got half way into New Mexico. The pass at
Raton, New Mexico was especially bad. I kept telling myself, "It's got to get better." Eventually it did. I
finally turned off the heater and opened the window
(no air conditioner.)

Mr. & Mrs. John Anderson from Scranton, North
Dakota, wintered in Tucson, Arizona, every year
so I headed there. They were happy to see someone
they knew and so was I. I stayed with them a couple
days. John showed me around Tucson and I looked
for some work. Not finding anything there I took off
for Phoenix. Between Tucson and Phoenix is a small
town of Florence. Near there is a road sign marking
the spot where Tom Mix was killed in a car accident.

I had never seen the desert before. I was fascinated with all the vegetation. It wasn't at all what I expected. I thought the desert would have very little growing on the vast stretches of sand. Of course I had seen pictures of the great saguaro cactus so that wasn't a surprise, but even these were much bigger than I expected. There was so many different types of cactus it would take a lifetime to learn the names of them all. Then there were the mesquite and various shrubs and bushes. Most all of them had thorns. I can see why the cowboys rode with heavy chaps and tapaderos on their saddles.

The birds and animals were different from what we see in the northern states, too. Most noticeable was the road runner, a long legged, slender-bodied bird that is built for speed. You see them frequently along the road and they can run really fast. There was also a type of rabbit I had never seen before. It didn't turn white in the winter, and a little fox they called the swift fox.

All in all I liked the desert, (in the winter.)

Traveling toward Phoenix I came to Apache Junction. At that time (1956) Apache Junction was one filling station and a curio shop and it was 30 miles to Mesa. Now the two have grown together. Between Apache Junction and Mesa I saw a rancher fixing fence near the side of the road so I pulled over and went to talk to him about the possibility of some work. He said he had just hired an Indian the day before as he was getting ready to gather his cattle to ship. I envied that Indian. A riding job was just what I was looking for. This was rough country in sight of the famous (or infamous) Superstition Mountains where so many prospectors disappeared. We had a nice little chat. He said his name was Weeks. I knew some ranchers in

North Dakota by that name so perhaps that is why I still remember his name. He said he had 100 sections of land and could run 300 cows. 100 sections in North Dakota would run 2000 or more. He said they were in a drought and were having to burn the spines off of cactus with a torch so the cattle could eat the cactus. He said feed was so scarce that some ranches hadn't turned the bulls out with the cows for two years so the cows would survive. They were afraid the cows wouldn't live and feed a calf, too.

The weather on the desert is very unpredictable. It can be in a drought cycle for a prolonged period and all of a sudden a cloud burst will come. When it rains, the desert turns lush with all sorts of vegetation including wild flowers of all colors and shades. Then without warning a hot wind comes up and everything dries up again.

I went on to Phoenix and stopped at one of the 3 sales barns. I was told to go to talk to the auctioneer, he might have some work. He said he owned a sale barn in Wilcox, Arizona, and he needed some help. So I went to Wilcox. Wilcox was not a big town which suited me fine. Hotel rooms were $2 a night or $10 a week. The rooms were pretty plain with only a small gas heater for heat. You didn't dare use the heater for more than a few minutes at a time because they weren't vented.

I went to check out this sale barn just out of Wilcox and a sign caught my eye. It said, "Sale Ever Thursday" instead of every Thursday. That was good enough for me. A lot of people would say it like that, especially in the south.

I talked to the man that owned the barn. When I told him I was from North Dakota, he said I could work for him. His son-in-law was managing the yards so I was to report to him. This wasn't a very big sales yard, but quite new. It was built with pretty light material so those desert cattle would crash through the pens. So he put me to patching broken pens. Then on sale day (every Thursday) we all had to sort cattle and help with the sale.

They had a black man helping me. He was probably in his 30's and the funniest man I ever knew. He made me laugh at everything he said.

That was a lot of laughing because he talked continually. I can't remember his name but he had an interesting past. He had been playing poker with some fellows when he got in an argument over a $1 bet so he shot the guy. He went to prison where he found religion and was released to start his own church in Wilcox. He didn't have many parishioners so he needed a day job, too. He wasn't much used to doing that kind of work but he was willing. His job was to be my gofer. When he thought I might need a board, he would say, "Do you need a bode? I'll get you a bode." I enjoyed having him around.

Cattle were handled a little different at this barn than any I had been at or worked at. When the cattle were worked for the brand inspection, they were each run through a chute instead of reading the brands as they ran down the alley. The brand inspector brushed the brand site with a brush. He said he could see the brands better that way.

The first sale day that I worked we had a fairly big consignment of calves from one owner. They were Brahman calves and a nice uniform bunch so I ran them all in at once. The ring man sent them all back and told me they wanted them one at a time. It didn't seem sensible to me but that's the way they sold them.

Wilcox was and still is a small town. I liked it there. People were really friendly. I suppose everyone knew I was a stranger, but folks would talk to me on the street or in the cafes and when they found out I was from North Dakota they would make a remark about how cold it must be up there in the winter time. They could somehow believe that people actually lived in South Dakota but never in North Dakota. That was just too far north to be habitable.

One day I was sorting some cattle to go in the ring to be sold and a rancher came up to me and asked if I wanted a steady job on a ranch. I told him I did but I didn't have time to talk to him until after the sale. Actually I only wanted a steady job until spring but I didn't tell him that but I think he figured I was only south for the winter. Anyway he told me to come to his headquarters if I was interested and that night I did. He lived in the foothills of the Graham Mountains near Safford.

He offered me a job taking care of a bunch of calves at a camp not far from Wilcox. This camp was where he wintered his calves after weaning and the young man he had working there wasn't working out so I was to replace him. I felt sorry for him. He had no idea he was being replaced until I drove in the yard. He had a new wife and they both looked like teenagers. I hope he didn't have too much trouble finding another job.

Average wage for a cowboy at that time was $125 a month and a place to sleep. We furnished our own groceries, bedroll and saddle. Not much money but I was in the south where it was warm doing the kind of work I enjoyed.

The cabin I had was pretty bare. The cook stove was electric and there was a table and a single cot with no mattress. No heating stove of any kind and there was a path instead of a bath. The running water ran up an open irrigation ditch and then I pumped it up to an overhead tank and then it gravity fed down to the one faucet in the kitchen. Even though it was Arizona, it froze at night quite often so my running water would be frozen until about 9:00 o'clock each morning. I would run a bucket of water at night so I could have coffee for breakfast.

I did my own cooking, of course. I ate a lot of eggs, bacon, cornbread and beans. As long as I was living in the south, I thought I should eat southern cowboy grub.

The ranch was owned by a man named Dee Jernigan. He was a typical ranch man and looked the part. He migrated from Mexico many years earlier. He ran mostly Hereford cattle, but also had a small herd of Texas Longhorns. (More about Longhorns later.) There were 50 sections of land and since it was partly in the mountains, they got more moisture than down on the desert so he could run 300 mother cows. Then with this irrigated feed base he could grow the calves out after weaning. Calves don't weigh as much down there at weaning time as they do further north. Of course that was in 1956 and calves didn't weigh as much in the north then either.

In that big country where cattle can move around a lot they tend to become a little wilder, a little more suspicious of humans. Sometimes a smart old cow will take her calf and go hide in the mesquite when it's weaning time. So the calf doesn't get weaned but a smart cow will wean the calf herself but maybe a little later. Sometimes these calves will avoid capture for a couple years. Mr. Jernigan would capture one of these renegades from time to time and bring them down for me to care for. He would also bring down some cull cows to get a little fleshier before they would go to market. Some of these older cows would refuse to eat or drink for 2 or 3 days. They would stand and bawl and look back at the mountains. Eventually they would start to eat. Mr. Jernigan told me he has seen cows starve to death because of homesickness.

One problem that was quite prominent on this place, especially with older steers, was water belly. That is when a kidney stone obstructs the passage of urine. When that happens, the stone must be surgically removed. There is a more scientific word for this common ailment, but I never can remember it. It is fairly easy to detect the symptoms. The steer becomes very uncomfortable, switches his tail a lot and his belly becomes distended. Surgery must be done soon so the bladder does not rupture.

It is not a very complicated surgery but Mr. Jernigan told me to call the vet if I noticed a case. I was glad of that. I don't like to do that kind of surgery on someone else's livestock. I had 2 cases that winter and I called the vet and we saved them both. I had to go to the neighbors to make the call. There was no phone at camp. (No cell phones those days.)

There was no chute to catch cattle with on this place, just a big pen (which suited me fine.) There was a one-eyed paint stud there for me to ride so I saddled him and roped the sick steer. When I laid a trip on him and rode off, I could tell this horse had done this before. When the steer went down, I had plenty time to get off and tie him. This horse was really pretty except for the one eye gone and Dee told me he had been the Arizona state reining champion some years before this.

I liked Arizona and I made some friends there. I can't remember any names now, but I remember one cowboy in particular. His name might have been Adkins or Askins, but maybe not. He was working for the O-O ranch about 20 miles from my camp. I met him in town one Saturday night and we got to be good friends. He was batching, too, and his job was mostly to break horses. The ranch was owned by absentee owners. He liked to rope, too, and there was an arena at his camp. I went up to rope with him a couple of Sundays, but all there was to ride was the green colts he was breaking. One of them bucked me off and broke my tail bone. That hurt bad all spring. I was wishing I could have used the one eyed stud but I didn't have a horse trailer or permission to take him anywhere.

I started home about the middle of March. It was time to start calving

My old Chevy was running pretty good in spite of the fact I had to add a quart of oil every time I gassed up. I hadn't saved any money while I as in the south but I figured if I didn't eat in restaurants or sleep in motels, I had enough to buy gas and oil. It took me 3 days to drive home. The speed limit was 55 m.p.h. then and besides if I drove over 50, my car would use even more oil so I kept it down.

At night I would pull off the road where it seemed sort of quiet. I would find a little wood to build a small fire to cook my supper and then I'd roll out my bed and sleep for a while. Towards morning it would be pretty chilly so I'd get up early and cook a little breakfast and get an early start.

With all the crime you hear about now days, I don't believe I'd feel safe camping beside the road now, but I did then.

I went by the Grand Canyon on the way home that time. I had never seen it before. I was certainly impressed. I was used to seeing canyons in the badlands of North Dakota but this was unbelievable.

When I got back to the ranch, I had 9 cents in my pocket but I was home where the bankers knew me and I could borrow some operating money. It was good to be home. It had been a relatively mild winter and Wilmer managed very well without me. The livestock, cattle, sheep, and horses, looked good.

Chapter 14

Some Horses

I went to a few amateur rodeos the spring of 1956 and it became apparent I needed a better horse. I saw an ad in the local paper for a registered thoroughbred stud. He was 4 years old and been used on cattle. I bought him from Bob Swanke at Marmarth, North Dakota. He was the first registered horse I ever owned. His name was Chance Flag. His sire was American Flag who was spirited away from his home in Austria because when Hitler began invading those countries, the good thoroughbred and Lipizzaner horses were in danger of being killed. American Flag became the property of the U.S. Army remount. Chance Flag was also a remount horse. When the army remount was disbanded, the horses were all sold and John Harstad bought him and brought him to Rosebud, Montana. He later sold him to Bob Swanke and I bought him from Bob. He was a good dependable ranch horse, followed cattle good and didn't bother other horses even though he was a stud.

He hadn't been used in rodeos much so he didn't know much about barriers but then I didn't either so we learned together, I guess, but maybe not much. This was in the 1950's and there weren't as many registered horses being used then as there is now. There were a few purebred quarter horse studs but few mares were purebred so most horses were out of grade mares and by purebred sires.

Not long after I got Chance, I took him to an amateur rodeo in Belfield, North Dakota. I wrote about that earlier.

If I had a job to do horseback, Chance would get it done whether it was running horses, gathering cattle, cutting cattle or dragging calves to the branding fire, he would do it with ease and never get excited. The only problem was when it was time to rodeo, it was also time to breed mares. I believe studs should run in the pasture with mares at that time so it was inconvenient to travel with a horse you had to go to the pasture for each time you wanted to go to a rodeo which at that time of year was most every weekend.

When I saw the first crop of colts sired by Chance, I was disappointed in the quality so I decided to sell him.

I had some other saddle horses that were good ranch horses and would do anything a ranch horse should do, but I thought I needed something a little faster for competition so I went shopping again. Ernie Singletary from Dickinson was shipping good horses into North Dakota from Texas. He was in business with Punch Oglevie, a trainer from Texas. Punch would come to Dickinson with the horses and help Ernie sell them. These were good quality quarter horses and Punch had them working really well in calf roping and reining. I picked out a good looking

4 year old buckskin gelding. He cost me $400 which was a high price in those days. Today a horse like him and trained the way he was would no doubt cost a few thousand.

I hauled him to rodeos and horse shows for several years. He was good for me and several other ropers would use him. Tiny Engesser was at a rodeo in the little town of Lodge Pole, South Dakota and his horse was lame, so he rode old Buck. Tiny was a better calf roper than I was so he beat me that day, too. Years later whenever we would meet, he would say, "Do you remember the time I borrowed your horse and beat you in the calf roping?" How could I forget? Tiny was a good hand and a good athlete. We team roped together some and he also mugged for me in the wild cow milking. I preferred roping with him rather than against him.

Buck wasn't quite 20 years old when he contacted sleeping sickness and had to be put down. That was a sad day. He ran so many steers and calves and was a good pleasure horse and also a good ranch horse. One consolation - I didn't have to pension him off and watch him get old and stiff and perhaps die in a snow bank.

One morning I was getting ready to go to a branding at the Logging Camp Ranch. I wasn't going to take Buck that day, because he had a minor wire cut on a front foot and I wanted it to heal up before I used him again. I had gotten a different horse in and grained him and had him ready to load but didn't load him yet as I wanted to get some breakfast. I had everything ready to go including backing the truck up to a little bank so the horse could jump in. (No horse trailers those days.) Buck was running loose around the yard and when I came out after breakfast, here he was standing in the back of the truck. He wanted to go to the branding, too. When I left with the other horse, Buck trotted along beside the truck whinnying.

Branding time was fun time in western North Dakota when I was a kid. Neighbors would get together and brand each other's calves, (as they still do today). No one had more calves than could be branded in one day because there was always a big enough crew to get the job done. Days would start about sunup with the gathering and corralling the cows and calves. Some owners wanted the cows and calves separated when the work started and some left them stay together. The owner of the cattle was the boss when his herd was being worked.

Most ranches now days still brand the old and best way. The calves are roped by the hind feet, (heeled) and dragged to the fire where a pair of wrestlers throw them down and hold them while the person with the hot iron brands them.

Mechanical contraptions have been invented to hold the calf, but I detest that method and they aren't very widely used in ranch country.

I enjoyed all aspects of branding and did them all from time to time such as wrestling calves, branding, castrating, vaccinating -- but of course if I was lucky enough to get to rope that was best of all. Then when the work was all done, there was beer and a big meal. The camaraderie was great. It was a good time for neighbors to get together.

Shipping time was of course another time of year we looked forward to. Sometimes a buyer would come to the ranch and make an offer to buy the calves or yearlings or whatever we had for sale each fall. If we didn't make a deal with a buyer, the stock would go to a terminal such as Sioux City or they would go to the local sales ring.

Chapter 15

The Wedding

Wilmer and I ran the ranch together for nine years and I would have to say it was a happy time for me. By that time Wilmer and Grace had their four children and they needed more than half a ranch. Rose Marie and I were planning to tie the knot so the plan was for Wilmer to take over the ranch and Rose Marie and I would relocate somewhere else. We decided on Glendive, Montana, where Rose Marie got a job teaching high school English and I set up a saddle shop. Glendive had been without a saddle shop for several years so it was encouraging when people said they appreciated having one in town.

Since Rose Marie was brought up Catholic and I remained Lutheran, I had to have a meeting with the priest who was to marry us. I was a little nervous about that but Father soon took care of that for me. The first thing he said was, "I suppose you think we're going to try to make you join the Catholic Church, but we don't even want you. We've got enough bad Catholics the way it is." I sort of took a liking to him. I also had to have a series of instructions by a Catholic priest. So I asked Father Fahnlander from Home on the Range if he would do it for me. We had become friends when he brought some of the boys to the theater to help. We got along really well.

Our wedding party.
Left to Right: Dad, Tex Appledorn, JoAnn Farrington, Me, Rose Marie, Mother and Freda Goetz.

The ceremony was in the Catholic Church in Harvey, North Dakota, Rose Marie's home town. The reception was at her mother's home. Tex Appledorn was my best man and Rose Marie's sister JoAnn was her Maid of Honor. Rose Marie's father passed away when she was 5 years old, so her cousin Gussie Kaibel gave her away at the altar. Everything went very nicely all day and we spent the night in Mandan. I had made arrangement for a bottle of champagne and flowers to be in the room when we got there. It was quite romantic. The next day we took our time getting to Amidon for the wedding dance and then to Medora to get to work at Old Four Eyes. We didn't get to have a honeymoon until the next summer when we went to Glacier Park.

Cutting our wedding cake.

Chapter 16

The Store

I wanted to start a saddle shop in Glendive, Montana, and I was able to rent space reasonably on the lower end of main street from Roland Utterback. Roland owned the Stockman's Bar and my space was next door to it. Sometimes late in the day the noise penetrated through the wall pretty loud. Occasionally a drunk would walk in my shop by mistake.

I had quite a few used saddles (and tack to go with them) that we used in Medora and I put them up for sale. I had enough tools and I bought some leather and sheep skin on credit and I was in business.

I started to get some repair work and also some orders for tooled belts and billfolds. Salesmen started to show up with merchandise and before long I had a western wear store besides the shop. After a year I moved to a bigger space that I rented from Freddie Dalsasso next to his barbershop. I also hired a high school girl to work part time. Judy Austby, Judy Walker and Gail Nagel all worked for me part time and then Sally Athas worked pretty much full time for a while.

Business was good. Many people would come in just to tell me they liked having a western store in town and would buy something before they left. I sold quite a few boots. That was before tenny runners and hat sales were good before baseball caps. Times do change.

I enjoyed being in business. My customers were 99% good, generous, and friendly people. The other 1% was OK, too, but could be a challenge from time to time. But that's human nature.

I depended a lot on salesmen to guide me in the right direction for buying merchandise. Most of them were conscientious about what to sell me and how much. It wasn't hard to tell when one would come by and try

The first saddle I ever made. It was back for routine repair in 2005.

to sell me things that wouldn't sell or to encourage me to buy too much. That happened very seldom. I appreciated the good honest ones. One of my favorites was from Taos, New Mexico. He sold Taos moccasins. The first time he stopped he only let me order 1 dozen moccasins. They were popular with ladies those days and I later increased my inventory considerably. After a couple years the salesman told me I as in the top ten for volume sales in his territory of 7 states.

Another salesman I really liked was Bill from Montana Leather Co. At that time the company was at Butte, Montana, but has since moved to Billings. Bill was an older fellow and a down to earth sort of guy that I liked from the first time I met him. He was very helpful if there was anything I needed but would never high pressure me into buying anything I didn't need.

I still buy from Montana Leather Co., but of course, Bill is not there. Instead there is John and Doug and they are both great guys and run a good wholesale business.

Me with two saddles I made.

Rose Marie was teaching English and speech at the high school in Glendive then and getting along very well. She liked the Montana kids and they liked her. She established discipline right from the start so she had very little trouble. She also directed plays those first years. She had a way of getting the kids to be actors. Some still talk about how much fun they had doing plays. After a few years at the high school Rose Marie moved on to teach at the Community College here in Glendive. Many of her former students have told me they really enjoyed her classes and learned a lot too. I was known as Mrs. Aus' husband.

When we first moved to Glendive, we rented a one bedroom upstairs apartment. I had never lived in town except for the four years I lived in the dormitory while in high school and it was pretty crowded. But everything was new and different. Getting used to married life and getting the business started and Rose Marie in a new school was all new and wonderful.

One day Cal Wyse came in the store and asked me if we would like to live in the country. He had a little place just four miles from town with a house and small barn and he would rent it to us. That was just about the best news I had heard since we moved to Glendive, but I told him I'd have to check with the bride. Rose Marie had never lived in the country and was pretty apprehensive about it. She was afraid she would become bored, but she said she was willing to give it a try. She was a good sport. So we moved to the country and after a couple days Rose Marie stepped outside and gave a big "yahoo". That tickled me and I knew then we would be country folks from then on. It was an older house and barn, but Cal let us keep a couple horses so we were happy newlyweds.

The place we rented from Cal was on Deer Creek which has a long drainage and when it rained or when the snow melted in the spring, the creek would flood. We didn't have to cross the creek to get to the highway, but there was a broad low area between the house and road that would flood. We drove a Volkswagen beetle those days and the water would get so deep the car would float down stream. When the water was too high for the VW, we would drive the pickup. Sometimes I would take the fan belt off to keep the engine from drowning out.

One fourth of July we had a cloudburst and the creek came up higher than I had ever seen it. Ralph Nelson and I were entered in a roping in Sidney on the fifth, but I didn't dare cross the high water so Ralph came with his trailer and I rode across. The water was about 6 inches above the stirrups. We were young then and it was all pretty exciting. We never missed a day of work because of high water.

Rose Marie kept on teaching and I ran the store. I intended to build saddles, too, but with taking care of the repair work that came in and taking care of customers and doing the book work, I didn't find the time to build new ones. But things always seem to work out. One day Niel McGrady, an old friend and saddle maker from North Dakota, came in the store and I was able to hire him. He was a good saddle maker and also a silversmith and an easy guy to get along with. He stayed with me until I sold the store and then he stayed with the new owners.

One day I was talking to Bob Schall, the Academic Dean at DCC. We discussed the possibility of teaching a class in saddle making. It would be an adjunct night class one night a week. It would be worth three college credits and we would need a minimum of seven students. The students would furnish their own tools and materials and would make a saddle or any other tack of their own choosing. Since I still bought tools and material wholesale I would give the students a discount on whatever they needed.

So we got on the schedule and had twelve students the first quarter. At first most of the students were older non-traditional students. Most of them built saddles for themselves but some of them chose to learn what they could by making smaller items like breast collars and headstalls.

Traditional students, both men and women, eventually started taking the course. Many were on the rodeo team and almost all were from farms or ranches. Almost all of my students were eager to learn but of course there were a few who found it hard to get to class regularly. Those I encouraged to drop the class so I didn't have to give them a failing grade.

I had several students who did very nice work and went on to produce saddles in their spare time. I thought perhaps I was a better teacher than saddle maker. I used to tell the folks in class, "Do as I say not as I do."

I taught saddle making for a total of 15 years at DCC and also a class for adult education in Circle, Montana, for several years. So that meant three hours a night twice a week. I enjoyed teaching but because of my illness in 1999 I was forced to terminate that aspect of my life.

I still keep my shop in the basement of our home. I do mostly repair work now but recently a fellow from Pennsylvania asked me if I would build him a saddle. He wanted one a little fancy. I wanted to say no but it came out yes. I had intended that the one I built for my nephew Gordon would be the last one in my saddle making career. But so it goes. Joe Marisa will be able to tell his friends in Pennsylvania that his saddle was made by an 81 year old saddle maker. (I've had another birthday since I started this little project.)

A friend named Cy Wyse stopped by the other day and talked about a new saddle so I'll postpone my retirement.

I made this saddle for our good friend Bob Metcalf. He and his wife Peggy secretly entered it in the Montana Winter Fair. When we arrived for the Fair, I was surprised to see my saddle with a first place ribbon.

Chapter 17

Kristin & the Big Blizzard

After being married a couple years we decided it was time to start a family. The baby was due in January of 1965. On December 14th 1964, eastern Montana had the worst blizzard in many years. It snowed and blew for 3 days and of course we couldn't get out of the yard. If we could have gotten out, we couldn't have seen the road anyway. Since Rose Marie was nearly full term, we were studying a book on child birth. Fortunately, we didn't need our new knowledge.

I had a little Ford tractor with a blade on the front so I was able to plow a track out to the highway after the wind went down and the sun came out.

Kristin was born about 8:00 p.m. on January 30th. After I left the hospital and went down town to pass out a few cigars, the wind started to blow. I made it home, but just barely and the next day I was snowed in again. By that time the snow was just too deep and too crusted for my little snow plow but the county plow came and did a good job and we didn't have any more trouble that winter. But it was a cold, miserable and long winter. The old house we were renting in the country was not insulated and it was pretty hard to heat. The kitchen was particularly hard to keep warm. The pipes for the sink froze every night. In the mornings I would have to thaw them out using a vacuum cleaner in reverse to blow warm air under the sink. That was just a little inconvenience for the chance to live in the country.

Rose Marie had resigned her position as English teacher at the high school and was planning to stay home with our new baby. Dick Starr was president of Dawson Community College then and he saw Rose Marie at the fair that year. He said he couldn't find anyone to teach English and would she be willing to come and fill the position until he could find someone. He said being pregnant wouldn't be a problem at the college level.

In January Rose Marie found an old friend from Harvey, North Dakota, (Kerry Murphy), to come and teach her classes. He arrived two weeks before Kristin was born and stayed for the rest of the year. She found him in San Diego where he was getting out of the Army.

When Rose Marie went back to teaching, Sally Athas came out to take care of Kristin. Sally was a wonderful second mother to Kristin and Kristin really loved her. She would bring her little son David with her and Kristin loved him, too. He was about 4 or 5 then.

One morning during the spring thaw, the creek was up over the road. It was high enough I didn't think

Sally should try crossing it with her car. I watched for her so I could meet her on the other side with my pickup. But before I could get there, she had taken her shoes off and rolled up her pant legs and was wading knee deep in icy water. I told her never to do that again. She said she didn't think she would, but that's how dedicated she was. She had worked for me in the store so we knew she would be good for Kristin.

Chapter 18

The Hillebrand Ranch

In 1963 I sold my interest in the ranch in North Dakota to Wilmer and bought the Langshaw place between Glendive and Lindsay. It was all grass but it wasn't a good place to winter cows. There was no protection from storms but it was cheap and I got some mineral rights with it.

The next year I sold it and bought the Hillebrand place S. E. of Circle on the west side of the Red Water divide. This was 7 1/2 sections and a well balanced ranch with good grass, plenty water and some of the best winter protection in the country. The improvements were almost non-existent and the road in from the Glendive side was just a trail.

About that time Rose Marie was asked to teach full time at the college in Glendive so we didn't move out to the ranch. We stayed at Cal Wyse's place and I drove out to work the ranch after I sold the store to a couple from Wisconsin. Ed and Doris Ellestad were the new owners and they ran a nice clean business for many years. I was glad someone would take over the inventory so Glendive would still have a saddlery.

I didn't have quite enough cattle to fully stock the ranch so I bought the cattle that Mr. Hillebrand had. They weren't very good quality cattle but I bought them right and I thought it would be good to have some cattle that were located on the place. Then I would mix some of mine in with them and hope they would locate on the new place. I also bought a couple hundred sheep from Hillebrand.

Heinie Hildebrand was in poor health. He suffered from emphysema so it was hard for him to run the ranch. He hadn't taken his bulls up and they were running with the cows all winter. When we closed the deal on the ranch and we took over, I went out horseback to pick up the two bulls. They seemed like gentle cattle when we drove out to look at them, but it was a different story when I showed up on a horse. The minute the cattle saw me coming, their heads and tails went up and they high-tailed it for a big brushy coulee. I could see I wasn't going to have any luck cowboying so I went back to the house and got the pickup and a stock trailer and a sack of pellets. When the cattle saw me coming this time, they came to meet me. I dumped a little cake behind the trailer where I had tied a rope. When the bull got close enough, I roped him. He fought pretty hard for a while but eventually gave up and I put another rope on him and dallied to the front of the trailer and kept taking up slack until he had to go in.

The next day I did the same thing and got the second bull. These cattle were broke to eat cake but not to be handled horseback—what we called drive broke. Eventually I learned bits and pieces of the story as to why the cattle were so afraid of a horseback rider. I put the story together and came up with this conclusion. Since Heinie couldn't ride himself, he had to hire his riding done whenever he wanted to brand or gather to ship. There were a lot of brushy coulees where the cattle could hide. The brush and trees were too thick to ride through so the cowboys would throw firecrackers into the draws to scare the cattle out. When they got them out in the open, they would run them hard towards the corrals. The theory was to push them so fast they wouldn't turn and head for the brush again. It was like running wild horses.

It took a lot of cow psychology to get those cattle so I could handle them. I put some gentle cattle with them and rode amongst them a lot. When they finally quieted down some, I picked out a few head and followed them a short distance and then let them go again.

By branding time that spring I was able to get a few at a time to the branding pen. I didn't ask anyone to help me because I thought the sight of more than one rider would intimidate them and all my efforts at training them would be lost. So when I was lucky enough to get some cows and calves in the pen, Rose Marie and I would brand those and turn them out again. Eventually we got all the calves branded. Rose Marie was pregnant that summer so she didn't enjoy branding much. That next fall I sold the wildest of the Hildebrand cows. Some just didn't want to quiet down like domestic cattle should.

There was about 400 acres of farm land on the Hildebrand place but I didn't feel I had the time to take care of the livestock, fix fence and put up hay

and be a farmer, too. So I rented that part to neighbor
Earl Green. I didn't know a lot about grain farming
anyway and Earl did a good job.

In early 1965 I decided to try for a real estate license so I could sell property for others. I thought I
could run the ranch and sell real estate too. I had
talked to Al Erickson of Erickson-Nielson Agency
in Glendive and he said I could work for them but I
would have to pass a pretty tough exam so I'd better
start to study. So I bought a book on the subject and
began to study. I was confident I could pass the test
because I had bought and sold real property so I at
least knew the terminology.

When it was time to go to Helena to take the test I
took the train. That was a good method of travel because it allowed me to cram for the test like we used
to do in high school. There must have been close to
50 people there to take the test. It was in the Capitol
building. The man giving the test told us before we
started that 60% would be a passing grade but not
to get to confident because 50% of us would fail. We
were allowed 8 hours to complete the test. I needed
the full 8 hours and when I finished I wasn't near
as confident as I was at the beginning. I passed, and
what a relief.

Over the years I've sold a few ranches and farms
and some residential property. Very few sales have
gone entirely smooth and easy. If both the buyer and
seller have hired a lawyer there might be a problem.
Each lawyer wants to do something for his client.
There doesn't seem to be any lazy lawyers.

Now and then we hear of a shady real estate salesman. Most are honest but one bad apple will spoil it
for the rest of us. I think perhaps that is the case
with most professions. I tell people that are thinking

of getting into the real estate business that as soon as you get a license you have a reputation to overcome.

I started selling for Erickson-Nielson Agency. We still had the ranch near Circle so I'd get up early and go to the ranch and do the chores and usually get to the office by 11 a.m.

After a year or so Bob Nielson bought Al Erickson out and it became The Bob Nielson Agency. Later Ken Kubesh bought out Bob Nielson and changed the name to Realty One. A few more years Ken sold the agency to Jane Bowles and Vonda Cody. After I sold a ranch for them I decided I'd quit. But Ward Fenton invited me to hang my license in his office so I did. This is going on 41 years for me in the real estate business. Ward and Alice Fenton and their daughter Paige have been our good friends for many years going back to the years when we were competitors at Appaloosa horse shows. Ward is also an internationally known horse show judge.

Chapter 19

We Moved To Belgrade

After operating the Hildebrand ranch for 4 years, we decided to sell out in eastern Montana. Real Estate values had begun to go higher and I was able to sell for a profit. Had I known how land values would continue to rise, I would have done much better by holding on to it for a few years, maybe I should have known better, but I didn't.

The plan was to go to Bozeman where Rose Marie could pursue a Masters degree at M.S.U. Then when that was accomplished, we would head for a new location in a warmer climate. We bought a small irrigated farm south of Belgrade, Montana. I sold the sheep we had but kept 150 head of cattle and moved them to Belgrade.

The house on this place we bought needed a lot of work so I played carpenter that winter besides feeding the cattle and a dozen horses. Kristin was three and I had her with me a lot of the time. I taught her to steer the pickup while I fed. I also audited a couple animal science courses at M.S.U. I found the courses very informative. I would have probably taken more if I would have had the time.

We were the last house on a side road off Cameron Bridge Road. We soon found out it was a favorite road for college couples to drive on late at night. Just beyond the house was an open field with some trees. Some of the young couples would park with their heater and radio on until the battery was run down and the motor would quit. Some would drive in and get stuck in a snow drift. Several times that winter there was a knock on the door in the middle of the night. Sometimes it was 25 or 30 below, but I had to get up and go rescue the love birds. One especially cold night I pulled a couple out of a snow drift and when the fellow was able to drive out, he came and said he didn't have any money to pay me for helping him, but he had a cold beer he would give me. I declined.

Another bitter cold night I rescued another couple. This gentleman also said he couldn't pay me but he was a hairdresser and offered to do Rose Marie's hair for her. She took advantage of that offer. She said she was well satisfied with his work. So that turned out alright.

Rose Marie graduated with her Masters degree after a year of hard work and long hours of study. Kristin spent some of her days at a day nursery on the M.S.U. campus. The first day there she spotted a rocking horse. She immediately got on it and never left it for 1 1/2 hours. The people taking care of the children were college students who were studying child behavior. One thing they were watching was attention span. They said no child had an attention span of more than 15 minutes so they were pretty amazed when Kristin stayed on the horse for an hour and a half. She was 3 years old then.

By the time Rose Marie had accomplished the reason for coming to Bozeman I had our little place pretty well shaped up and ready to sell. So that's what we did. I sold the calves and some of the cows early and shipped the rest of the cows back to Glendive to some rented pasture. We packed up and headed south to look for a new location. We tried to find a spot where there was an opening for a college English teacher and where we could buy a suitable ranch.

We looked at places in South Dakota, Wyoming, Colorado, and New Mexico. Nothing we looked at seemed any better than eastern Montana. We gave up on the idea and headed back to Glendive, where we bought a ranch north of Glendive from Bud and June Mahoney. After we closed the deal, we took off for old Mexico for some R & R. We went as far as Monteray Mexico where we stayed for a couple of days. We shopped and took in the sights and relaxed. It happened to be Kristin's 4th birthday, so we had a cake at the hotel. The Mexican waiters made quite a fuss over Kristin. They would touch her blonde hair and giggle. We had a good time but driving in the interior of Mexico then was quite an experience so we were glad to get back in the good old U.S. of A. Truck drivers thought they were the king of the road and would drive accordingly. On busy sections there would be three lanes of traffic going each way even though it seemed to me there was room for only two and then here would come a motor cycle and slip in between two trucks and speed away.

On the way back we came by way of Las Vegas. We had never been there before. We met our good friends

John and Sally Athas and Dan and Norma Peterson. Jeanne C. Riley was popular those days with her one big hit "Harper Valley P.T.A". She was singing there so we bought tickets and went to her concert. We stayed a few days and saw more concerts, ate a lot and gambled like we were spending our last nickel. One day John and I had a conversation with the famous Bennie Binion. In addition to the Horse Shoe Club he owned one of the biggest ranches in Montana, near Jordan.

When we got back to Glendive, we took possession of the Mahoney ranch. That was 35 years ago and we're still here.

We picked a good time to be gone from eastern Montana that winter. John Konig was taking care of our cattle while we were gone. I called to see how he was getting along one night in January. He said, "Merle, you son of a gun, you get back here. It was 52 below this morning." He was kidding, of course

Kristin at 4 years old.

Chapter 20

The Mahoney Ranch

We moved into the house and I immediately started to play carpenter again. The house was 3 rooms and no insulation. The first thing I did was build a little nest for Kristin. She was a happy child and everything was fine with her. I then insulated and replaced the inside cardboard on the walls with sheet rock. A year or two later we hired Jim Rahr, a local contractor, to build an addition on the house for another bedroom. Now Kristin could have a regular bedroom with her own bath. Jim Hyde laid the cement block for the new basement. When the addition was finished, I resided the house with cedar board and batten. The place took on a new look. Then we built a roping arena. A lot of friends came out to help build that. There was Niel McGrady, Ralph and Natalie Nelson, John and Sally Athas, Dan and Norma Peterson and Gene Pederson. I'm sure I'm forgetting some. When we were through building the arena, I bought some Mexican steers and we practiced roping.

A couple more years went by and we hired John Kron to build a large pole type barn with an alley big enough to ride colts in during the winter.

The original homesteader on this ranch was a Norwegian sailor by the name of Andrew Anderson. I've been told he jumped ship when he got to America and came to Montana. He worked for another Norwegian, Ivan Kalberg, who was already well established and had put together a good sized ranch on Morgan Creek. They ran mostly sheep.

Andrew decided to homestead some land on his own on Lower 7 Mile Creek. He told me the first year or so he lived in a cave under a rock ledge. That qualified for a dwelling to prove up on his homestead. The government rules were you had to live on the land and break up a certain number of acres of sod. After 5 years the land was free to the homesteader.

Andrew married Sena and built a small house across the creek from his dugout. They had no children, but a lot of friends. Everyone that came to their place was invited in for some homemade wine. The two of them worked hard and prospered, mostly with sheep.

They had lived on the place for 52 years when they sold the place to Bud and June Mahoney and moved into Glendive. Bud Mahoney was bothered with asthma so after 5 years they went back to Arizona where the desert air was better for him. When we bought the place and started to make improvements, Andrew was so happy. Whenever I saw him in a crowd, he would tell everyone how well I was taking care of his place. We got to be good friends even though I tried to avoid his home made wine. Norwegians stick together, I guess.

After we had lived on the Mahoney place for about 10 years, we decided we wanted to build a new house. We wanted more room. After much discussion we decided to sell the house and outbuildings, the arena, and some acreage and start a new set of improvements on a new location. We found a spot just up the creek about 3/4 mile.

Bob and Mildred Anderson had been living on some acreage not far from us but right on Highway 16. Bob had told me they would rather be a little farther from the highway so I offered to sell them our buildings and about 100 acres. We made a deal and were glad the Andersons were going to be our close neighbors. Their daughter Nancy is about 2 years older than Kristin and liked horses, too. The two of them traveled to some horse shows together. Bob and Millie also have a son Jeff who is a little younger and likes to travel on a bicycle. He even rides it to town, 12 miles. He keeps in good physical condition. He also likes to raise a garden and is a hunter and fisherman.

When Andersons bought our place, they sold theirs to Jack and Georgia Gannon who sold their place on Highland Park Road. Everyone had to give possession at the same time to make the deal work. That gave everyone a new place to live except us. I was involved in the whole thing as a realtor.

We hurried and hired Mike and Larry Haggerty to drill a well and got a septic system put in and then bought a trailer house to live in while we got a house built.

Kristin was 14 that summer and had taken some colts to ride besides some we had of our own. I think it was six head she was riding. We didn't have a barn or any corrals to put them in so she would hobble them at night until we got the barn partly up and made some temporary stalls with portable panels.

Jack Stout was an old cowboy who had worked around eastern Montana when he was a young man, then he went back east and worked as a carpenter for 20 years before coming back to Glendive to build houses. I was able to hire him to build a house and a barn.

When he agreed to come to work, I told him I wanted to pay him by the hour so if I didn't like his work, I could fire him. That didn't bother him, so he started on the barn first. I liked his work and he was extremely fast. He preferred to work alone but some things he didn't like to do, such as insulating and finish work. That was ok with me, so I was able to save some money by doing that part. Otherwise I stayed out of his way.

When I was in high school, I took 3 years of shop which included woodwork, carpentry and mechanical drawing. The knowledge I gained in shop has been very valuable to me all through life. I did a lot of re-modeling on the various ranches we bought and later resold. When we built the new house, I was able to lay the hardwood floor as well as doing most of the inside trim work.

When it was time to start on the house, I contracted the plumbing and electrical work done and Jack kept on building. We got to be good friends with Jack and also with the electricians, Lloyd Quinnell and his son Chuck. We hired a dear old friend from Bozeman, Bob Metcalf, to build a fireplace. He and his wife Peggy were horse show friends and we had many good times with them. They were special friends that we will never forget.

Rose Marie had been studying house plans for a couple years so she knew pretty much what she wanted. Sometimes Jack would object to certain things, but if Rose Marie had a fresh pie made she could talk him into anything.

Jack Stout's last name suited him. He was really stout, and he was also tough. Cold weather didn't bother him. He shingled the house in January, wearing a plaid flannel shirt, a leather vest and cowboy hat and worked bare-handed.

Jack was an interesting fellow and a great story teller. He had been a cowboy before World War II and rode the rough string on roundups on some big ranches south of Miles City. On one roundup he broke his ankle. Since he couldn't ride then they had him drive the chuck wagon.

A few years after he finished building for us, he and a girl friend stopped at our place for a visit. He said he was showing Doris some of the houses he had built around the neighborhood. While we were drinking coffee that day he mentioned that he had bought a head stone for his grave. We were quite shocked. He looked healthy enough and we hadn't heard that he had been ill. Then he asked if we wanted to hear him sing. We had no idea he had such a beautiful voice and he knew the songs from broadway hit musicals, pretty good for an old roughneck cowboy like Jack.

A few weeks later we got word that Jack had died and was buried and his headstone marked his grave. We lost a good friend.

The first painting contractor we hired to paint the interior of the house tried to raise the price after we had agreed on a price and after he had started the work. We had a falling out as they say and I told him to leave. I guess you can't win them all. We then hired three ladies, Cycelia Goosen, Elaine Goosen, and Fayette Miller and they did an excellent job. They also finished the oak kitchen cabinets that were built by Walt's Cabinet Shop in Dickinson.

We moved in then even though I had yet to lay the hardwood floor in the living room and dining room. I worked at that each night until I finally got it done. I still had a stair railing to build and a lot of trim around windows and doors when a horse kicked me in the leg and broke it. So I was in a cast for several weeks but I hobbled around and kept plugging away. We were certainly glad to get out of that little trailer house and into our new house where we had more room. Rose Marie did a good job planning the house. It's about 2700 sq. ft. with 3 bedrooms, 3 baths and a small office. Now that we have lived in it for 25 years., it's so full of stuff we wonder if we should have built it bigger.

They say a house never gets completely done and by the time you think it is, it's time to start doing some repairs. But all in all we are happy in our home and we had fun building it. Some folks say building a home is hard on a marriage, but I can't say it was hard for us to get along while we built ours. We enjoyed seeing the progress from day to day.

Later from time to time we did some small projects like corrals and a deck and some brick work on the front of the house. It was 20 years before we tackled another big building project. We decided to build a 3 car garage. I called my friend Herb Weiss. He and his helper, Jerry Schmidt, came out and put up the shell and hung the doors. Good neighbors Bob Anderson and George Darrah helped me put up the sheeting and I put in the windows. Rose Marie helped me with the siding and George helped me with the electrical work. Bruce did a good job on the floor.

The house and barn Jack Stout built. We still live in this house.

We like having a garage so much we wonder why it took so long for us to decide to build it. We have made good use of the barn, too. We have 6 box stalls, a tack room, a grain bin and on one end there is a shop. Also there is storage room for one of the buggies.

The Mahony ranch lies next to the Kalberg ranch. It is a good sized ranch established before 1900 by a Norwegian immigrant. Ivan Kalberg came to raise sheep. When we moved to the community Ivan was past 90 years old and in good health. His son Lars was managing the ranch and was running mostly cattle but also had a small band of sheep.

There was a bunch of wild horses running on the Kalberg range. They were descendents of some sort of draft breed going back many years. Lars kept them for coyote bait because the coyotes were killing his sheep. The predator control people would kill a few horses and inject the meat with the chemical 1080. This chemical has been banned since then so there is no longer a need for the wild horses. Lars sold them all to Bob Abernathy, a rodeo stock contractor, from Beach, North Dakota. These horses had never been touched. The studs had never been gelded. Their range was close to our fence so we saw them quite a lot. It was interesting to watch the studs fight each other over who should be in charge of the mares. There weren't enough mares to go around so the strongest studs got the most mares.

The county road ran though their range so they were accustomed to seeing traffic but if they saw a rider they would hightail it. They could run for 5 or 6 miles without coming to a fence. The narrowest bit of range was as they would go by our place which was a mile wide. Bob thought if a few riders would bring the herd up 7 Mile creek towards our arena we could corral them there. About 200 yards from the arena was a very steep and high bank. The plan was to bring the wild horses up between the bank and the arena and someone would be waiting there to turn them into the arena. I was appointed to do that. So I positioned myself and waited for the thundering herd. Bob had several friends from the Beach and Sentinel Butte area to help with the roundup. The ones I remember are Alvin, Tom and Ted Tescher, Jim Cook and Don Abernathy. They were about a mile away when I saw them coming as fast as these heavy horses could run. They paid little attention to me when they got to where I was supposed to turn them into the arena. Instead they split and went by me on both sides and went up the side of that bank that was supposed to be too steep to scale, like they had wings. Not only did they run up the bank but they ran up where it was the steepest.

I was riding a big black Appaloosa horse who got interested in the chase so I let him follow. It felt like he would tip over backwards but he made it to the top. The other riders were right behind and out of the corner of my eye I saw Tom and Ted take down their ropes so I did too. The wild horses were fairly winded by then so we were each able to rope one and bring them to the arena. The herd went west where they could go for 2 ½ miles. Jim Cook said he would haze them back and we could rope some more. So we caught three more that day. We castrated the studs and loaded them into Bobs truck.

Wild horses are like coyotes. They are smart and they are lucky.

After a couple more failed attempts they were all eventually captured. I heard that Jim Baisch went out and spent some time just herding them instead of chasing them hard and trying to outrun them. Patience pays.

Lars' nephew, Sam Undem is running the Kalberg ranch now and the wild horses are gone. In their place are some well bred Quarter horses.

It was fun to watch the wild ones but I'm glad they're gone.

Chapter 21

Some Horse Shows

Ihad always been involved in horse shows as well as rodeos, both as a competitor and as a producer. So we were pleased when at a very early age Kristin took an interest in showing horses.

We had been raising and showing Appaloosa horses and we liked the people we met at Appaloosa horse shows.

We raised some horses that did fairly well in the halter classes and I bought a big black horse with a blanket that was pretty hard to beat in western pleasure. I won quite a few shows but if Laura Brest was there, I sometimes had to take 2nd. Not necessarily because she had a better horse, but because she was a more skillful rider. Kristin also did well in the lead line class on this horse.

The Canadian National Appaloosa Show was held in Regina, Saskatchewan one year so we thought we might as well go since Regina is only about 250 miles from Glendive. It was a big show with horses from all over Canada as well as several from the U.S.A.

Joe was in his prime then and did very well. The Canadians gave very nice trophies and Kristin won 7 of them even though it appeared someone had drugged Joe the night after the 1st day of competition. When we went to feed the second morning, Joe was sweating and acted very hyper. I had never had any experience with that sort of thing. I didn't dare to report it or call a vet for fear of being accused of using drugs on the horse, which is illegal. It was early in the morning when we discovered the problem and her first class that day was at noon. He was obviously uncomfortable in his stall so I took him out with another horse we had along on a hunch he might settle down. At first he would try to rear and buck and kick, not at all acting his normal self. Three hours later he was

Me winning the Western Pleasure class on Black Nugget A in Billings.

showing signs of quieting down and by noon he was back to normal and Kristin won her next class.

We also had a feed bucket and some grooming tools stolen out of Joe's stall. That sort of thing was certainly not what we expected. We had never encountered anything like that before or since. Anyway we came home with a bunch of trophies and some cash. We always got along fine with other competitors. In fact, we were more like one big family. Many people we met during our horse showing days are still good friends.

The National Appaloosa Horse Club of America holds a worldwide show each fall. To be eligible to compete in the world show, you have to win 1st or 2nd in your region for the year in the event you wish to enter at the world show. Kristin qualified in several events but the high school administration wouldn't give her permission to be absent from school so she would have

Kristin in Leadline on Blackie.

had several days of unexcused absences. So we sent the horse to Oklahoma City to the show with Leroy and Sherri Anderson from Bridger, who would be going anyway. We hired a friend, Phil Luman, to ride Joe and the Gruwells from Selicia sent a good horse down and had Glen Hough ride him. Phil and Glen are a couple of the best team ropers in the country. They won the World with no trouble. So Kristin has a big trophy from the World Appaloosa Show. Rose Marie and I were especially proud because we bred and raised the horse right here on the ranch, and except for 45 days riding by Marvin Ley, Kristin did the training. We were competing against horses that were sold for many, many thousands of dollars and were trained by high dollar professional trainers.

The horse club sponsored an award ceremony for winners of the World Show and for the owners of the horses that won. This was held in Mexico City. For

Apache Joe A and Kristin at the Canadian Nationals in Regina.

this the school administration relaxed their rules and gave Kristin an excuse from her classes. She was lucky enough to go with Ward and Alice Fenton and their daughter Paige. Paige was the same age as Kristin and a very good rider. The two of them competed against each other for many years and are still the best of friends. Both are now in education.

The fun and excitement of going to horse shows, except for the local fair, ended when Kristin headed off to Carroll College in the fall of 1983. So getting a World Champion trophy and a trip to Mexico City was a fitting climax to several years of hard work and training a good horse that we raised in our own breeding program. We were proud of Kristin and Joe.

But Apache Joe didn't get to retire just yet. Instead he became my top heeling horse, replacing Square Butte who was getting old and deserved a rest.

Chapter 22

Slope County Fair and Rodeo

I had been on the Fair Board in Slope County for a few years and of course I kept promoting a rodeo. But first there had to be an arena built. I got some opposition from the other members because of the cost. So we started out slow. The first year we built one little pen and a small chute and offered kids calf riding. That went over well so the next year we expanded and had cow riding for bigger people. The third year we added calf roping.

The Saddle Club had made a little money by putting on play days around the country and did some entertaining with the quadrille team so we approached the fair board to let us build an arena and put on a rodeo. We got permission from the fair board, so we set out to buy some cheap material. We found some used railroad ties and some old rusty woven wire. Bob Hanson went to Ashland and got some cheap rough lumber and we were ready to build. I put a notice in the local paper that an arena was to be built at the fair grounds and we needed help. On the appointed day 35 men showed up with hammers and saws. We had an arena before dark. Max Wilson was the building foreman and he kept people working.

The club put on the rodeo the 1st year, but after that the Fair Board took over and eventually the rodeo was sanctioned by the North Dakota Rodeo Association (N.D.R.A.) I was on the Board of Directors of the N.D.R.A but when I moved to Montana I was no longer eligible to serve.

The old arena that the club and community built that day has long since been replaced by a very nice modern facility. The Amidon Fair is going strong with a rodeo every year. It's fun to go back at fair time and see all the old timers that show up. The club had a big part in getting a rodeo started at the Slope County Fair and since I was the president of the club and also on the fair board, I like to think that I had a little part in helping to make it happen.

Chapter 23

Dad & the Auction Sales

Dad liked to go to livestock sales. He was always in the front row at the sale in Bowman every Monday. He liked to buy both horses and cattle. Buying horses in those years wasn't usually very profitable but it was a hobby for him and he enjoyed it. One time he bought a Shetland mare with a mule foal at side. It was a cute little black mule. At weaning time I thought I'd halter break her. That turned out to be fairly difficult. I had never worked with a mule before. I found out they have a little different temperament than horses. Being half Shetland didn't help any. I turned her out in the fall, thinking I would continue her education later when I had some free time but I found her after hunting season. She had been killed by a hunter's bullet. That was the only time in my life that I had anything to do with a mule. Some people really like to work with mules. They seem to be smarter than horses. Maybe that was my problem. The trainer has to be smarter than the trainee. I was glad Dad came home with only one mule.

Dad bought and sold cattle regularly at the Bowman sales ring. Not on a big scale. His strategy was to buy odds and ends, usually one at a time that would sell cheap. Maybe because they were off colored or otherwise didn't fit in with others in a bunch. He would turn them out to pasture and soon he would have a load that would match up and also would have some weight gain.

I still had a small truck from my former trucking enterprise so when Dad had a load of cattle ready, he would tell me and I would take the truck and a saddle horse to his place and we would gather a load that looked alike and haul them to the Bowman auction.

The loading chute was about 1 1/2 miles from the pasture so we would hold the herd against the fence not too far from the gate. Then we would sort off the ones he wanted to sell one at a time and put them out the gate. With just the two of us horseback we had to keep the herd from getting riled up so mostly we never got our horses out of a walk. Dad was a genius at working cattle quietly and calmly. He could read what a cow was going to do. With a horse that had a little cow sense and a little handle, he could put a cow right up a tree. Well, maybe not quite, but there was never any doubt that we wouldn't get to the corral with what we wanted and the cattle wouldn't be at all disturbed. In the fall he would have a load coming and going nearly every week. He was tall and he rode straight in the saddle with a little belly touching the saddle horn. He rode until he was past 80 years old.

Les Wilhelm from the Halliday, North Dakota, area leased a ranch north of Amidon for a couple of years. He had some cattle of his own and pastured some for Frank Hoff of Richardton, North Dakota. When Hoff was ready to move his cattle back to Richardton in the fall, Les asked Curt and me to help gather. Les' cattle were running with the Hoff cattle so they had to be separated. This ranch had been used for sheep for many years so there were no corrals suitable to hold that many cattle, so when we had the cattle all rounded up we moved them to a large flat where there was a fence we could hold the cattle up against. Les and Frank did the cutting, one at a time making sure each cow had her own calf with her, and making sure the brands were right. Hoff had a brother that helped Curt and me hold the herd and the cut. I believe there was one more rider but I can't remember who it was. Anyway the whole operation went without a hitch. It was fun to work with good hands and good horses. They needed help the next morning so Curt and I stayed over night. The ranch house wasn't big enough for everyone so Curt and I slept in an old scale house at a coal mine near by. There was no heat in that old house but we had plenty of good heavy quilts so we slept like babies.

In the early days of our ranching careers at Amidon, Wilmer, Dad and I had quite a bunch of semi-wild horses (usually about 40 to 60 head.) If we needed to pen them for any reason, we had to chase them a couple miles to a corral. That was different from working cattle as the first thing a bunch of horses would do is run, so you had to run and head them in the right direction. On a long trip, they would eventually slow down but just a couple miles, they would still have plenty of run left. Wilmer was a good hand with horses, too. He was breaking horses to ride when I was just learning to ride (about 5.) When he and I would go to corral a bunch of horses, we would often be out of sight of each other. We would both know where the horses might make a break for it and would try to be there to head them off. If I couldn't see Wilmer, I would worry that he would be too late and the horses would get away. I should never have worried because Wilmer was never late. He would always show up just in the nick of time and be at the right place. Running horses was fun and exciting. A good stout horse that had been getting some grain was a real asset in running horses. A saddle horse that had been fed a little grain for a couple of weeks would have a lot more stamina than one that had just been grazing. Oats is a good horse feed but sometimes corn is fed. Also barley and speltz can be fed. My dad told me speltz was a very good horse feed, but it's not as readily available.

Dad sold a semi load of mares to a trucker from New England, North Dakota. I think his name was Paulsrude. He was buying mares for shipment to Missouri and other southern states where they were bred to Jacks to produce mules. So we corralled a bunch of horses to load in his semi trailer. In the herd that we corralled was a really good looking gelding. He was 2 years old and pretty wild. While we were sorting horses to load, this gelding jumped over the corral wall and got away. This was such a good look-ing horse and obviously he was athletic, that I thought I should own him and make him a saddle horse. So I bought him from Dad

He ran with the other range horses for another year and I decided it was time to start breaking him. When I tried to get him to the corral he would quit the herd and run off by himself. I tried to pen him several times, with other horses and also by himself. The big problem was when he came to a fence he would jump over it and then I had to hunt for a gate to follow him. It was a miracle he didn't get wire cut. He stayed a free horse for another year. He would usually show up back with his own band but finally he started to stay by himself.

I needed a horse whisperer but at that time I had never heard of one. So I thought of a plan of my own. He had taken to staying in a pasture on the north end of the ranch. There were three fences between the pasture and the corral at the ranch. I opened the first gate and hobbled a mare just on the other side of the fence close to the gate. The next day I went back and found the gelding had taken the bait. So I closed the gate and moved the mare though the next gate. By proceeding in this way I eventually got him in a pen too high for him to jump and then to the round pen which I had built higher just for him. By now my plan for his future had changed. I made a deal with Avon Lester who was buying bucking horse prospects. I let him know the horse was in and he could come and get him.

Avon came with a truck with a high stock rack. His son Mike was with him. Mike stayed in the cab ready to drive away as soon as we got him loaded. When the horse decided to go up the loading ramp and into the truck he was running hard. When he hit the truck bed with his front feet he made a big leap to go over the side but Avon was waiting for him on the ground with a long pole and persuaded him to stay in the truck. I managed to slam the tail gate shut and Avon yelled to Mike to take off. Mike let the clutch out and goosed the motor to jerk the horse off his feet.

Then he slammed on his brakes to throw him down again. He did that several times until the horse gave up trying to jump over the side. Avon ran and jumped in with Mike and away went my pretty sorrel gelding. I saw Avon in town later and he said he made it home but his stock rack was pretty much demolished. He said whenever they met a car or truck the horse would kick at the side of the rack.

Russ Alexander raised a horse with a similar attitude. When this horse saw someone coming he would run to the top of the highest hill and blow and whistle. He was a Paint gelding and very attractive when he stood on a hill with his head and tail in the air. I wish we could have had a movie of him. Unlike the sorrel this horse had a respect for fences so we thought we could run him down to catch him. Russ wanted to break him to ride.

One Sunday afternoon Bob Hanson, Marvin Ryan, Curt, Russ and I rode out to capture the wild horse. The plan was for one rider to run the horse until his horse was winded and then another rider would run him. He would soon be winded enough so someone could ride up on him and rope him. It worked and we put two ropes on him and went to Russ' corral.

The horse didn't seem to gentle down much but Russ had him halter broke and figured he might as well get to riding him. He asked me if I would snub him the first time he got on him. The idea was to try to keep him from bucking if we could or at least keeping him from bucking hard. Bob and the hired man, (Marvin) were batching at the Logging Camp ranch for a few days so Russ and I thought we would go spend the night with them and Russ would ride his bronc. After a pretty rough start where Russ got a bloody nose we got along good and I turned Russ and the paint horse loose and we made the 6 or so miles to the Logging Camp a little before dark. I don't remember what become of the pretty paint horse but I remember Russ rode him some that summer and then his uncle Jack from California came and rode him quite a bit. It could be that Jack took him back to California with him. The horse never seemed to get gentle, but that didn't bother Jack.

Chapter 24

Music

Ever since I can remember, Wilmer could play the harmonica. Since I always tried to imitate him, I was trying to play at an early age. I was making a little headway when I was about 6 years old. People would ask me to play. At that age you aren't expected to be very good. Unfortunately I didn't get much better.

I was about 10 years old the summer my oldest sister Blanche and her husband K.C. Smith visited us as they were moving from Austin, Minnesota, to Wenachee, Washington. K.C. had a small button key board accordion. I really coveted that instrument. When they were packing up to move on, I noticed he had not packed up his accordion. I knew I should tell him he was forgetting it, but I didn't. I was feeling guilty about it but then I heard Mother tell him. Then I was relieved when I heard him say, "I haven't forgotten it. Merle will get more use out of it than I will."

I was able to squeeze a little music out of it and I sure enjoyed it. I'm sure the folks were tired of all the noise, but they were very tolerant and didn't ever tell me to quit. I didn't know many songs then because we didn't have a radio and of course TV was many years in the future. So I imagine I played the few songs I knew over and over. Still the folks didn't seem to mind.

Thelma's husband Lloyd Deitz was a very talented musician and had a good singing voice as well. When we got together, he would play the mandolin or harmonica or he would play the guitar and sing. I learned a few old time cowboy songs from him. We also had an old time phonograph with a few records. Strawberry Roan was one record we had.

The country schools around the area had P.T.A. meetings once a month. Sometimes I was asked to play the accordion at these meetings. Not that I was good, but because I was so young, I didn't have to be good.

One night at a P.T.A. meeting, they had invited an old time fiddler to play. I thought that had to be the best music that I was ever going to hear in my life. I wish I could remember the old gentleman's name and the tune he played. He was a farmer from north of Scranton. That farmer and his fiddle made such an impression on me that I couldn't help but bug the folks for a fiddle. I knew there wasn't any money for such things, but I couldn't help but talk about it.

Some time later Dad sold a horse to a fellow who had an old violin and was able to get it thrown in on the deal. I was really surprised and happy. This was an old instrument with a crack and no hair in the bow. I managed to pull some hair out of a horse's tail and fixed the bow. I got a hold of a little resin and I was ready to saw away.

I thought I was doing pretty well on the fiddle but when Lloyd heard me play, he said I wasn't fingering it just right. I decided I didn't have a good enough ear for an instrument that didn't have the frets marked so I gave up on the fiddle and went back to the accordion and harmonica. I got a harmonica holder so I could play both at once.

When I graduated from the eighth grade, there was a county-wide graduation ceremony. I was invited to play the accordion. That was probably the highlight of my musical career.

When I was a senior in high school at Augustana Academy, I found a used mandolin in a music store. It was marked $4.00 so when I got $4 for doing odd jobs around town, I bought it. Orville Munson was a good buddy, who also lived in the dorm and he had a guitar. We would get together in a dorm room and play. We sure had fun. Sometimes we even had an audience. After graduation we each went our separate ways and didn't see each other until our 50th class reunion. We were able to play together again and even cut a tape. What a thrill after all those years.

After I graduated from high school and Wilmer got out of the army, he got a banjo and then a guitar. We spent many evenings playing together. He has a better ear for music than I have, but we played mostly for our own enjoyment so it didn't have to be perfect. Occasionally we would be asked to entertain at various functions around the country but nothing professional.

After I got married and moved to Montana and Rose Marie got on the faculty at DCC, I played with Myron Damon. He was also on the faculty and also played the guitar professionally. We would play at faculty parties. I don't know what he thought of playing with an amateur like me but I sure enjoyed it and he was a good sport.

Myron left the college to go to Minot, N.D. after a couple years. Then John Gibson, also a professor at the college, played a guitar so we continued to have music at the faculty parties. In those days the faculty, staff, and administration was like one big happy family. There were fewer people involved then so it was different.

John Gibson died a few years later, so then I didn't have anyone to play with and I just didn't play much after that. Now and then I pick up the mandolin or banjo, but after 20 or 25 years, I'm pretty rusty. Neither Wilmer nor I ever had any lessons and don't read music. Wilmer kept up with his guitar and harmonica and also taught himself to play the keyboard.

The music they write nowadays is much different than the old time country music we played 50 years ago. The young folks like it. I can't say that I do. I guess I'm just old-fashioned.

Wilmer and me playing together.

Chapter 25

Politics

In 1984 the Dawson County Democrats were looking for someone to run against the incumbent Republican for County Commissioner. I hadn't been involved in politics before. In fact, until the Richard Nixon fiasco I wasn't sure I was a Republican or a Democrat. Anyway I threw my hat in the ring as a Democrat.

I campaigned quite a bit that summer and fall and people told me I would be a shoo-in. I should not have listened. When the votes were counted, I was 252 votes short. Out of 2530 votes, that was pretty close, but close doesn't count in an election. I just didn't campaign hard enough. Dawson County has been pretty much a Republican county, so it's been hard for a Democrat to win, but I don't blame anyone but myself. I had good support from a lot of people, just not quite enough.

I have good friends and relatives who generally vote the Republican ticket. I seldom discuss politics with them if I think it will turn into an argument.

I respect their right to an opinion and hope they respect mine. I don't think either party has all the good people with a corner on all the bright minds. I happen to think the Democrats work for the betterment of the common people and don't cater to the rich. Teddy Roosevelt was a Republican, but he worked hard to make life better for the working class such as coal miners and other laborers. I admired him for that. He fought against big business mergers that would create huge railroad and oil company monopolies. He was not always in good standing with his party but he fought for what he believed.

Another Roosevelt (F.D.R.) became President following President Hoover (a Republican). The big stock market crash happened during Hoover's administration. F.D.R. inherited the worst depression the U.S. has ever seen. But with all the public works projects people were able to feed their families and a lot of conservation work was done. Dams were built throughout the country as well as roads.

The Democrats have been called the tax and spend party. I believe the Republican party should be called the borrow and spend party. I believe we should not

My campaign picture.

spend money we don't have. I especially don't like borrowing from China who has lent us billions of dollars in the last few years. Ronald Reagan, the great communicator, got us into a sizable debt. The country got out of debt and had a surplus under the next Democratic administration. A lot of people don't want to give Bill Clinton credit for the surplus, but it did happen on his watch, whether you liked Clinton or not.

But it doesn't matter. George W. Bush gave it away and borrowed billions. He says he will get it back. I hope he does it soon.

Some good things have happened for working people when the Democrats have been in power. For one thing F.D.R. established the F.D.I.C. so that our bank deposits are insured and people will not lose their money should the banks go down like it did in 1929.

Rural electrification (R.E.A.) was also established by F.D.R. and what an improvement in rural life that is. Believe me, I was there when it happened.

But probably the most important thing for the working class people is Social Security. That was also established during F.D.R.s' administration. It not only provided for retirees so the elderly don't have to depend on their relatives for survival, but also provides assistance for widows with dependents and victims of hard luck.

President George W. Bush would like to partially privatize social security. That has not worked in countries that have tried it. I suspect it would be a mistake here, too. We are told it would cost trillions of dollars for the transition.

Our two party system of government has worked for over 200 years and although sometimes it may seem like it is about to fall apart, it has always been that way. I have read biographies of famous presidents of both parties and they tell of bitter partisan fights all through U.S. history. Debate is a good thing.

One thing I would like to see changed is campaign financing. No other country in the world spends so much money on campaigning.

I often wonder why some folks are Republican and some are Democrat. I believe some people choose a role model and come to follow that person, no matter what. The George W. Bush administration is not being very kind to people in agriculture, but many big ranchers and people in big corporate ranching are staunch Republican and certainly helped put him in office for the second time.

Ben Franklin said, "A person has no control over what he or she believes." He said that in the context of religion, but I think it might apply to politics as well. If there is a flicker of reality to that statement, then you don't have any control over what you believe and neither do I.

Chapter 26

Illness

In 1999 I was 74 years old and I thought in pretty good health. Kristin had made a sale on the internet for me of a cross-bred Halflinger gelding and I was to deliver it to Mandan. The buyer was a lady from Minnesota and she was to meet me at Kist Livestock.

When I got home from that trip, I started feeling lousy. I thought I had the flu and it was settling in my back. By the 4th day I could no longer get out of bed. I ended up in the hospital. For 2 weeks Dr. Battle tried to figure out the problem. He ordered a lot of tests, including an M.R.I. but the orthopedist said my back was ok. Just give it time. Dr. Battle had been on the phone with specialists in Billings and they finally decided I had developed endocarditis, a blood infection that damages the heart valves and then travels to other parts of the body. In my case it went to my back.

After they figured out what antibiotics would stop this particular bug, they put a tube in my arm and ran it up to my heart and then sent me home for Rose Marie to nurse back to health.

It was going to take six weeks of heavy duty anti-biotics to cure the infection. Then the back could be attended to. The drugs came in large plastic bags that hung on a pole above me so it could drip into the tube in my arm. At first I was to get 9 bags of the fluid per day. It took an hour for each bag to empty and it had to be watched so that when it got empty no air got in the line. An air bubble in a vein would be fatal. The fluid had to be administered at regular intervals day and night. This got to be a terrible burden on Rose Marie. She had to hook the bags up and unhook them while making sure everything was kept sterile. She just wasn't getting any rest and I was getting worried about her health. They were giving me two kinds of anti-biotics and it wasn't long before I had a reaction to one of them. So they had to find something else. The one they chose was a much more powerful (and more dangerous) drug but the good thing about that one was I only had to have 6 bags a day so it relieved Rose Marie just a tiny bit. She was a real trooper through all of this.

I had a lot of company while I was laid up. My good neighbor Bob, who was doing some haying for me, stopped every day. George and Sandy Darrah came often and kept the grass and weeds mowed around the house. Tom Kalloch also did some mowing. Pastor Paul and Avis came to bring me communion, Vern Heinrich tilled the garden, and Pat Moline did the shopping. All this I really appreciated and so did Rose Marie. She was confined to the house. Something she is not used to. She never complained but I know she had to be stressed out.

When I became sick, I was doing a real estate deal. I was selling a farm. When the sellers heard I was laid up, they came to see how I was doing. I appreciated that. I didn't know the lady very well and during the conversation she mentioned that what I had was serious and people died from it. I knew that, but I wasn't planning to do it right then. Thank you for that bit of information. So many people were praying for me God didn't have a choice but to get me back on my feet. When you are down and out, it is comforting to know your friends and relatives are asking for God's help.

Finally after six long weeks, the tests showed the infection was cleared up and now we could concentrate on fixing the back. Dr. Battle suggested I go to a bigger medical center. Kristin, Rose Marie and I discussed where to go and we decided to try Mayo Clinic in Rochester, Minnesota. Rose Marie's sisters Marian and Jo Ann pushed hard for Mayo too. I was a little reluctant because of the distance, but I'm glad now that we went there.

Rose Marie rented a van and George and Bob made a bed so I could lie down on the way. I could walk a short distance with a walker, but I couldn't sit for very long at a time. To go very far I needed a wheelchair. Kristin came from Bottineau, North Dakota, where she was teaching, to help with the driving.

As soon as I got to the clinic, I saw a neurologist and he put me right in the hospital, which was fine with us because it was hard for me to get around. I had to be pushed in a wheelchair. That day they immediately started doing tests. In fact, they were still doing tests at 10:30 Saturday night. When the doctor saw the results of the M.R.I., he could see I had compression fractures of 2 vertebrae and 2 discs were destroyed by the infection. It looked bad to me, but the doctor said, "We'll fix it."

More tests and they discovered the infection had seriously damaged the mitral valve in my heart. So I needed to have open heart surgery immediately. The surgeon who would be doing the operation said it was so bad that 60% of the blood was flowing back to my lungs instead of going to the brain. He said if it wasn't fixed right away, my heart would start to enlarge and that would be irreversible. I asked him if he was the best heart surgeon at Mayo. Just joking of course but he answered, "I'll get it done. I did 5 yesterday". He let us know he was no amateur. His name was Kenton Zehr and I had complete confidence he would "get it done." After he left the room Kristin said, "You wouldn't want a humble surgeon would you"?

The back people went to work and built me a turtle back brace to stabilize the back so the damaged portion of the spine could fuse together. With the brace I could walk again. I was sent home to rebuild using a treadmill. Our friends rallied around and helped every way they could.

Two weeks later I was ready for the surgery. It seemed to be just a routine thing for everyone involved so it was hard for me to work up any anxiety about the whole procedure.

The surgery went very well just like Dr. Zehr said it would. Instead of replacing the valve, he repaired it. He sewed it up with Gortex. He even built a new seat for it. He said it would last as long as I would need it. It's been seven years, so far so good.

My back bothers me a lot and my inner ear was damaged by the prolonged use of strong antibiotics. As a result my balance is so bad I don't dare get on a horse any more. That's a bit annoying, but I have ridden a good many miles for a lot of years and I'm thankful I can get around without help and can drive a vehicle. I have an ATV which serves me well but it's not much good for roping.

I went to see a specialist in Billings to see if anything could be done to improve my balance. He asked me to walk down the hall and back. He said with a chuckle that I walked like an old cowboy with a bad back. He then sent me to an ear specialist who said my inner ear was damaged either from the long term use of powerful antibiotics or from the infection and there was nothing to do to help it. He also said, "Count your blessings. Most people don't recover from endocarditis as well as you did." So that was sort of good news-bad news, but I can live with it. I'm lucky to be able to sit without pain and also lie comfortably. Maybe it's good to have an excuse for not doing hard work and riding colts any more, but I used to enjoy doing hard physical work.

Chapter 27

Grandstand Renovation

The grandstand at the Dawson County fairgrounds had deteriorated to the extent that it was a serious danger to anyone who came to watch a rodeo or any other event from the grandstand. In 2000 Bill Blankenship and Larry Nelson called a meeting of the community to plan the renovation. I have never seen a better response and here is a complete story of what happened written by Rose Marie for the Montana Horseman magazine and reprinted here with her permission.

A Grandstand Renovation
July 2000
By Rose Marie Aus

In March of 2000 a very small ad appeared in the Ranger-Review, Glendive's bi-weekly newspaper. The ad called the public to a meeting concerning the condition of the fairgrounds. KXGN radio and television both put out announcements – a very simple call to attend a meeting about the grandstand.

That night meeting organizers went after more and more chairs as fifty-five people entered the room.

This was a noteworthy response for a town with a population of 4600 in a county with a population of only 11,000.

The large attendance was probably inspired more by civic fear than by patriotism. In the summer of 1999 the local citizens had seen their grandstand condemned by the building inspector as unsafe. Then they heard rumors of someone, a thin woman, not a fat lady, falling through the decking.

Although the grandstand was disintegrating, the rodeo arena in front of the grandstand is newly redesigned, brightly painted, attractive. There was a real dichotomy: a fine arena to draw cowboys from all over and a condemned grandstand in front of it Even the optimists could see the potential for a lawsuit or, worse, the death of the Dawson County Fair.

The seriousness of the problem was summed up when, during the meeting, Bill Blankenship, one of the originators, felt compelled to say to the audience, "Don't mistake this. This is not a problem to be solved with a bake sale."

At that original March meeting people were asked to sign sheets putting themselves on one of three committees: project, work, or finance. Almost everyone signed something: some signed two. The committees met that night after the public meeting and designed a format and set dates. Soon Larry Nelson and Bill Blankenship, the originators, asked George Darrah to be the coordinator of the effort.

Each of these three brought something to the project. Nelson had years of downtown business experience, Darrah is a retired district engineer for U.S. West and Blankenship is a weekend rodeo pickup man who works as a brand inspector for a day job.

Immediately the work committee set about assessing the state of the building. This is a structure that is basically seating: some aluminum benches with backs and some backless wooden benches. At ground level there was an area with four large doors and 28 exhibit booths. Narrow storage ran along the whole building where it fronted the rodeo arena.

The first group from the meeting to visit the grandstand encountered deplorable conditions. A Rube Goldberg system of interior rain gutters had been constructed to collect and carry outside the water that ran through the decking.

Rot was everywhere, ceilings, walls, stairs. A day after the group inspection, demolition was scheduled. Typical of what was found was described by Bob Anderson, a chemical company engineer, now retired to a small ranch. He said, "I took my good crowbar thinking 'I hope I don't damage it' but when I got there I could use my old broom to sweep away most of the building"

Quickly it became obvious that this was rebuild more than repair. But volunteers appeared by the dozens and began work.

The volunteers are by no means all men. Women show up and get to work every day. Secretaries arrive saying, "Hey I'm on old 4-H kid.' One woman who works all day at the medical clinic works most evenings at the grandstand. She is rebuilding the place where 60 years ago, the seats were filled with race fans cheering her mother, who was one of the more competent jockeys.

The core of the volunteers was made up of young men, many from BNSF, who gave hundreds of hours. As soon as they got off work they came, maybe taking off a couple hours to watch a son's ball game, then back to work until dark. These are men of great skill and overwhelming generosity.

Soon after construction began the group of "geezers" formed. These were retired men in their 60s and 70s who possessed many skills useful to the project-construction, electrical, plumbing. They became so involved they began meeting under the grandstand every day after lunch and they made steady progress forming bonds of companionship based on mutual respect for their responsibility and capability. They worked away their summer setting aside their personal building projects and even vacations to replace the entire exhibition structure with new framing and fire code sheetrock, all perfataped and painted.

As the ground level was gutted and rebuilt the deck of the grandstand was being fortified with steel beams. That project needed some heavy duty assistance from local industry like Lufkin, Williston Basin, Border Steel, and U.S. West. Installing the 40 foot beams was a major task involving huge machines with skilled operators and expert welders.

These businesses with their regional or national bases have been very responsive to this community project. They show they value the little town where their workers live and they will donate valuable worker hours and powerful machines to improve the circumstances for their workers' families.

As the time rolled on and the Ranger-Review and KXGN gave the project more and more publicity and more and more workers showed up. One recently retired professional man, not a famous do-it-yourselfer, joined the group and now classifies himself as a "Journeyman Holder." That occupation is defined as a guy who holds and fetches things for the more skilled.

By the time of this writing, July 19th, over 4800 work hours had been volunteered, many by skilled men with demanding jobs who always find time for the grandstand. That is equivalent to 120 work weeks or almost 21/2 years from one man's life.

All this community spirit was noticed by owners of a business. They have a hand operated button machine and, in respect for the enthusiasm, designed and pressed out 710 buttons for grandstand support. The project committee talked it over and decided those should be "thank yous". So a group of women volunteers organized and walked, bicycled, and drove around Glendive giving out buttons and gratitude to everyone who had donated materials, cash or made a pledge. The buttons were a big hit and people wear them around town reminding the world of the grandstand project.

Presentation of a button often stimulated the receiver to tell a story about the fair. There are hundreds of stories here revealing why the fair is so important to such a broad spectrum of Dawson County's population.

A surprising response from the grandstand volunteers, one that is repeated frequently, is, "I'm getting to know so many nice people. We've lived here for years and never got to know each other. Now I find wonderful folks." Sweat pours down, muscles ache, home projects suffer neglect but the workers rearrange their lives daily to work for the whole county.

At that original meeting, an older couple didn't sign any of the three committee sheets but they dropped $50 and from then on it was like "ask for it, it'll come". Money came in the mail. A local banker took over as finance chair. Checks were left with the county treasurer, businessmen walked to the stores and offices suggesting 5 year pledges: the suggestions were readily agreed to. And the checks came and came.

A ballpark estimate was made that $175,000 could cover everything. The finance committee met for the first time in March. By April 19th they had $18,000. By May 19th they had $70,000. By July 19th they had $113,000. The bake sale mentality caught on. A grocery store gave away hot dogs and pop in their parking lot with donation jars prominently displayed. A video rental shop sold hot dogs. A car wash gave a whole day's, proceeds, $519. Expert quilters have made a special King sized quilt to raffle. They expect to raise thousands. The two lumber yards in Glendive poured out a steady stream of discounted materials. Cement delivered for cost. "A special friend" pressed $1000 into a committee chair's hand. An old widow living alone gave $500 and upon receiving her thank you button said "My husband loved the fair. If you get your back to the wall, if you're broke and the bills are coming, phone me"

The fairgrounds property is county owned. The county commissioners feel they aren't able to help in any way. Some county officials view the whole affair with purse-mouth disapproval. The $89,000 bill for the aluminum bleachers and aluminum decking on the floor is coming due as the truck sped toward Montana from the Texas factory. The project directors have decided that a note will be drawn on a local bank and the collateral will be personal signatures from county citizens-evidence of the faith people have that the funds will continue to come. When the plan for the loan was covered in the Ranger-Review people began calling the organizers to say "I sure want to sign that note." A rancher who spends his time sitting at the hospital bedside of his wife who is ill with cancer was the first to call, "My wife and I want to sign that note."

Checks began to come from out of town. One of Montana's real problems has been the exodus of its educated bright young people to places offering high paying jobs. Those youthful exports evidently harbor warm memories about the Dawson County Fair. Checks have come from a Boeing engineer whose family farmed in Dawson County, from a woman practicing law in Washington DC, from a son of a retired city worker now on the west coast, a kid who loved the fair. The year 2000 has been busy with class reunions in Glendive and the graduates have left personal contributions and sizable group donations. One morning as a crowd left the Catholic church, a woman reunion goer who left Glendive in 1954 and whose family is all gone pressed a large bill into a rancher's hand and said, "get this to the bleacher folks." Her older brother gave $1000.

As work fell into a pattern, Wednesday night became work night. Sandy Darrah who has been beside her husband every minute of this project began to call some groups and ask them to bring food out to the workers at six P.M. When news spread that meals were welcome on Wednesday night representatives of groups began to call Sandy. "Have you got a date for us?" Quickly groups volunteered all the meals for the entire project. Groups like Lions, Kiwanis, Zonta, churches like Methodists and Zion Lutherans, organizations like Cowbelles and 4-H clubs and workers associated at the work places like the staff at Dawson Community College, the staff at Community First Bank. People deliver meals for thirty people on Wednesday and call Sandy on Thursday asking, "Can we do this again?"

The grandstand sits next to another government building, a new regional prison. Although the prison is built with no views of any kind the noise of the workers must carry over the walls. Serious about doing good to the community, the inmates donated a variety of artistic work for sale with the proceeds to go entirely to the grandstand fund. Horsehair items such as hatbands and zipper pulls and watch fobs were made and donated. Drawings and paintings were donated and the Native American Culture Club made dream catchers for the sale. A particularly talented inmate designed a T-shirt to symbolize the project.

The new grandstand is far sturdier and thus safer than the old one. Not only will the exhibit area have the fire retardant sheetrock but upstairs the number of steal beams has been doubled from 18 to 36 and those beams have been extended to the ground offering more stability as well as more seating.

Examples abound of the quality of the work going into the building. In one instance, in a misguided attempt to shore up the building, someone years ago had added a beam too short for its purpose. A wooden block was nailed to the wall to catch the end of the beam. Now that's all been fixed.

At the first meeting Bill Blankenship looked at the crowd and said, "Don't mistake this. This is not a problem to be solved with a bake sale." Now he says, "I was right and I was wrong-this has been solved with a hundred bake sales."

Beyond a doubt the best improvement is the handicap accessibility.

Many Glendivians ask, "Why did this grandstand project so inspire this community? Only speculation can answer. Perhaps Glendive citizens feel their county has hit bottom with economic decline and low agricultural prices and the oil bust and it's time to start up. Maybe Dawson County loves its fair so much that they will fight and sacrifice for it. Perhaps people finally wearied of the constant whining. "There is no money: the tax base is eroded: the mill levy is down", and decided there are ways to solve problems using creativity, leadership and generosity rather than taxes.

The effects of the rebuilt grandstand will last for years. Glendive knows this is a truly unusual and impressive flowering of community spirit. Pulling together, seeing a great success, meeting new friends all makes for something even more precious than a beautiful building.

Rose Marie didn't give herself any credit in her story. She was the one who thought of calling the organization, "Fair For All". She was always present at planning meetings and she worked with Sandy organizing the Wednesday night meals. She and Sandy were also the thank you button chiefs.

Several years ago, with some encouragement from our neighbor Peggy Winchell, who was the librarian at the Glendive Public Library, Rose Marie organized some of her friends to form The Friends Of The Public Library. The library was in need of a new facility and the Friends were able to earn enough from fund raisers to hire a grant writer, Mary McDonough Garfield, who won a federal grant to buy the former First National Bank building for the library. Rose Marie is also active in other organizations in the community such as The American Association of University Women, (AAUW.) She is a former member of the Montana Committee for the Humanities, is active in the Democratic Party and was on the state Latigo scholarship committee. We call her the social director of Lower Seven Mile Creek.

I did a little carpenter work on the grandstand but was unable to do any heavy work. The group graciously appointed me the official photographer so that I could have a small part in the project. I took hundreds of photos of the work in progress and used the best ones in a photo album so we have a record of the accomplishments of a community with a spirit.

Dr. Martin Luther King, Jr., once said, "Service to a community is the rent we pay for the space we occupy." I believe a lot of folks-young and old-have paid a big portion of their rent by working on the grandstand.

The finished Dawson County Fairgrounds Grandstands.

Chapter 28

Texas Longhorns

I grew up thinking Hereford cattle was the only breed to have. They were more docile than some of the other breeds. Most of the neighbors in North Dakota had Herefords and a herd of Hereford cattle grazing out in the hills is certainly a pretty sight. The exotic breeds from Europe were not being imported yet so it was mostly Hereford, Angus, Shorthorn and a few Galloway and Brown Swiss as far as breeds were concerned.

Later on the Hereford cattle begin to have calving problems, prolapse problems and pink eye. In an effort to produce a short chunky animal, a problem with dwarfism showed up in some herds. I blame the purebred breeders for that. They have overcome those problems in recent years, but it hurt the reputation of the breed. A typical Hereford cow today will probably weigh at least 200 lb. more than it did 50 or 60 years ago. It also will have some pigment around the eyes to prevent pink eye. The purebred breeders of Hereford cattle have made a transition to a breed with fewer problems than years ago.

I didn't change with the times. I just changed breeds. I changed to raising registered Texas Longhorns. I started by buying 5 head of cows and a bull. The cows were bred when I got them and the first spring I got 3 bull calves and 2 heifers.

I bred some yearling Hereford heifers to the bull I bought and had no trouble calving them. I kept those calves along with the rest of the calves (as was my usual way) until they were yearlings. When I took the yearlings to the auction that fall, the crossbreds sold for 2¢ a lb. less than the straight Herefords but because of the highbred vigor the crossbreds weighed more so they brought $32 a head more then the straight Herefords.

So that convinced me. I sold the Herefords, took in a partner and bought more registered Longhorns. The demand for registered Longhorn cattle in 1980 was strong. A good young cow or bred heifer was bringing $2000 and up.

Lowell Davidson, Rose Marie's nephew, is a building contractor in Hawaii. He wanted to get in the cattle business so he and his wife Betty bought some Longhorns and we ran them with ours.

Rose Marie and I had Longhorns for nearly 20 years and really enjoyed them. Kristin was getting old enough and was good help, too. She was better help for me outside than she was for her mother in the house.

A lot of people would ask me why we raised Longhorns and what were they good for. I would tell them we raised them for the money. They would give me a funny look as much as to say I was pretty dumb to raise Longhorns when you can make so much more with some other breed. Maybe, but it didn't work that way for us. Our biggest market was for bulls. We sold yearling bulls to ranchers (mostly bigger operations) to breed to yearling heifers because the expected birth weight for the 1/2 Longhorn crossbred would be about 65 lbs. or less. The heifer would calve with no trouble, and with no help and the calf would jump right up and start sucking. That eliminates the need to get up every two hours during the night to check heifers. We had several good customers for bulls south of Miles City and also in Canada. Our Longhorn heifers ran with the older cows during calving and I would check them once a day.

Longhorn cattle mature a little slower than some other breeds. Also the calves are born lighter so at weaning time the calves are a little lighter. If the rancher held the calves over until they were year-lings, they would pretty well catch up and the buyers wouldn't discriminate as much.

Another market we had was for roping cattle. The Longhorns run faster and do not sour as quick as the heavier breeds. Some ropers prefer Corriente cattle, but Longhorns are fairly comparable. When the calves are too big to use in the calf roping, then they advance to the team roping.

When they are no longer suitable for team roping, they can go to the feed lot. When fattened, they are as good as beef gets. I feed several most every year. As I mentioned earlier, they are slower to mature but they eat less. I found that a steer weighing 800 to 1000 lbs. would eat about 12 pounds. of grain and gain about 2 or 3 pounds a day. I think that's pretty good feed conversion compared to other breeds. (If I fed much more than 12 pounds, they would go off feed.) I'm not an expert but the bottom line is the cost to produce a pound of meat. Are you production oriented or profit oriented? I raised Longhorns for the profit.

Some feeders feed barley to steers but I believe corn or oats produce a better tasting steak. It is very important to hang the beef carcass for at least 14 days before it is cut, wrapped and frozen.

People have asked me if Longhorns are hard on fences. I tell them not at all. If a Longhorn needs to get to the other side of a fence, they just jump over it. Like any other breed, an individual cow will get to be breachy. I'd like to say they aren't any harder to keep in than other breeds but that wouldn't be quite true. They are quite athletic and they do like to travel but if the fences are kept tight they are manageable. I usually nailed the top wire two or three inches higher than for other cattle.

One of our Longhorn Cows.

Another thing people asked me is, "Are they mean? They look mean with those horns." The answer is "not at all." I've seen a lot more Angus cows get on the fight then I have Longhorns. If a Longhorn sees something that disturbs her, she would rather depend on flight to get herself as far away as she can.

Are they wild? Not unless you make them wild. We had cows that would eat pellets out of my hand. I enjoyed working with these cattle. They seem to be more intelligent than some. When trailing Longhorns, you just have to get them moving and then keep them going in the right direction. They string out and keep moving instead of having to be pushed every step of the way. When you get to a gate or a corral, you need to give them time enough to look it over and let them decide to go in on their own. If you try to push them too fast, they will bolt and run.

When feeding cake to a bunch of Longhorns in rough country where they can't come straight across, they will find a way to go around an obstacle. The Herefords would just stand and bawl and you can honk and holler all you want, but they just stand and look dumb.

In the nearly 20 years we had Longhorns I helped one heifer give birth. That was because of a breach birth. The head was turned back. I had no cesareans and one case of pneumonia. Perhaps a light calf is better than a dry cow.

I was short a cow and calf one day so I went looking. I found them in the neighbor's pasture with some Angus cows. I tried to drive her toward home, but when the cow started running to try to get back to the black cows, the calf wouldn't follow. So I let the cow go wherever she wanted to go, which was back to the cows. I let her go at her own pace and the calf followed her. I kept following her and kept making her move. It wasn't too long before she figured out I wasn't going to stop pushing her and she took off for home at a slow trot with the calf at her heels. That little trick worked on a bull sometime later. That time neighbor Bob was riding with me. The two of us no doubt could have chased him home, but by letting him think it was his idea we didn't get him hot or on the fight. After following him a few minutes he took off for his own bunch of cows.

The Longhorn cattle in America have an interesting history. I once did some research for a talk I gave on this breed of cattle for the annual meeting of the Frontier Gateway Museum and also to a gathering at the Glendive Library. A lot of my information came from a book by J. Frank Dobie. He loved Longhorns and wrote quite a lot about them.

Christopher Columbus brought the first cattle to the new world on his second trip in 1493. He landed in Santa Domingo with a few Spanish cattle and some horses. In 1519 Gergoria de Villalobo brought horses to the mainland of Mexico and in 1521 he brought the first cattle to Mexico. Both cattle and horses prospered and multiplied.

A few years after Cortez conquered Mexico, Coronado gathered 500 head of cattle and a herd of horses and started north. At each creek or river crossing he would leave a cow and bull and a mare and stallion. A year later he reached what is now Texas. The cattle he left in the U.S. did not survive. They were killed by Indians. They did survive in Mexico and did well.

In 1690 cattle were again brought to American soil. This time they were brought by Spanish missionaries. By 1770 there were thousands of Longhorns in the southwest despite frequent Indian raids.

In 1769 a few cattle were brought to San Diego, California. There the Indians were more friendly than they were in Texas. J. Frank Dobie wrote, "Texas had Apache and Comanche. They were magnificent riders, but never submitted to baptism or rode as obedient herdsmen for Spanish tongued masters as did the Indians in California."

Soon there was a surplus of cattle in Texas but no market. Shanghi Pearce had the reputation for being arrogant and perhaps a little shady. He trailed a herd of cattle to the Gulf of Mexico to look for a market. There was no market for the meat there either. The cattle were butchered for their hides and tallow and the carcasses were dumped in the Gulf of Mexico. J. Frank Dobie said of Shanghi Pearce, "He was never molested by modesty".

When the Civil War broke out, the men abandoned their ranches and went to war. The cattle ran free and became so wild eastern hunters came to Texas and hunted the cattle like game animals.

After the war the ranchers came back to find millions of cattle on the range, but again no local market. So the trail herds started north to find better grass and a market. Many stories have been written about the dangers encountered by the cowboys on their trips north, some as far north as Montana and North Dakota. There were stampedes, Indian attacks, storms, and rattlesnakes.

Teddy Blue Abbot made several trips north with trail herds and later wrote a book about it. He called the book "We Headed Them North" and I really enjoyed reading it. The cowboys were reckless and carefree when they got to a town like Miles City. Thirty five hundred cowboys were reported to have made the trip. About $\frac{1}{3}$ were either African American or Mexican. A few were women and all were young. Many were teenagers.

It was a hard life for the cowboys and also for the cattle. Authorities on the subject have written that perhaps the Longhorn breed was certainly the best suited for such a long hard trip. Since the Longhorn cattle survived without any help from man, they evolved into a hardy breed because it was survival of the fittest. They grew immune to disease, the yellow fever ticks didn't bother them and if they had trouble giving birth, they died. J. Frank Dobie said it best, "They were bred not by man but shaped by nature and man benefited. Had they been registered, regulated, restrained and provided for by man they would not be what they have become". What they have become is a breed of cattle with high fertility, easy calving, disease and parasite resistance, hardiness, longevity, ability to utilize browse and coarse forage, and the ability to convert feed to muscle and fat with less back fat, more marbling and less cholesterol than other breeds. Longhorns cross well with faster gaining cattle and still retain their hardiness and other good characteristics.

I might also mention a strong mothering instinct. Coyotes don't have much of a chance to kill a calf from a Longhorn cow. It's not a good idea to let a dog follow when you're riding around cows with young calves.

Often I've seen one cow baby-sitting a bunch of calves while the rest of the mother cows went to water.

I'm sure there are plenty of readers who think what I've written about Longhorn cattle is not true, but there have been many trials to prove that Longhorns and especially cross breeds have done very well in the feed lots. They grade a big percentage of choice and some even prime. But most of all I know I had more live calves to sell, the cows wintered easier and cheaper and there was a good market for bulls. So the bottom line favored the Longhorns for us.

Perhaps there are people who wouldn't get along with Longhorns. A person who likes to whip and spur, holler and yell while working cattle probably wouldn't get along too well. Quiet and patience is usually the best way to work any breed of cattle.

Chapter 29

Montana Centennial Cattle Drive

Longhorn cattle showed up in large numbers In 1989 when Montana celebrated its 100th birthday as a state. Stan Lynde and Barry McWilliams, two famous cartoonists, thought up the idea of a real authentic cattle drive. There would be thousands of cattle trailed from Roundup, Montana, to Billings, Montana, a distance of about 50 miles. There would also be hundreds of horse-drawn wagons, as well as hundreds of riders on horseback. It would take a week to make the trip. Everyone would camp out. No one would be allowed to go to town during the whole week.

It sounded like fun. A lot of people were skeptical, including me. The logistics seemed impossible.

But there were meetings in towns all over the state explaining the details and choosing leaders in each community. Stan Lynde and Barry McWilliams had done a tremendous amount of work getting land owners permission to cross their property and getting corporate sponsors. It looked more feasible. Rose Marie said she'd like to go so we decided to go. We would find a team and wagon and go on "The Great Montana Centennial Cattle Drive." Kristin would go as our outrider.

It wasn't long before I saw an ad in the local paper for a covered wagon for sale in North Dakota. I believe the town was New Leipzig. We drove over to look at it and I could see it needed some work, but basically it was all there and it was being used the day we saw it. So we bought it and arranged for the delivery.

We still needed a team. One day my good friend Wally Badgett, who draws the cartoon called "Earl," called from Miles City. He needed a Longhorn bull to use on some heifers he had gotten from us previous to that year. In the course of the conversation, I was telling him about the planned cattle drive and that I needed a team. Wally said he just happened to have a nice team and he would trade his team and harness for a Longhorn bull. How lucky can you get! So we made the trade and we were set to go on a really big adventure. Well, almost ready, but not quite.

When the wagon was delivered and I got the team home, I decided I'd better go for a trial run. I hooked up and the team went great. By the time I got a quarter of a mile from home, a rim came off one of the back wheels. The weather had been dry and the wheels shrank and that's the way it is with wooden wagon wheels in dry country. I remember my dad used to soak his wagon wheels in the creek every once in awhile when there was a dry spell.

Well, I unhooked Poppy and Slug and walked home with them. I went back with a pickup and some tools to put the rim back on and some baling wire to keep it on till I got home. Then I started to look at my new purchase a little more closely. In fact, I looked it over a lot more closely. I ended up taking it apart piece by piece. Wherever there was a bolt going through the wood, it was loose because of old dead wood. So I took everything apart. The bolster, axles, skeins and anything I could and scraped down to solid wood. Then I used that modern invention fiber glass to replace the dead wood I had scraped off. That tightened up everything. I also used fiber glass to tighten the rims, but I also bolted them to the fellows (the round wooden part that is next to the iron rims) so we had a good wagon in good shape to start the trip. I also had Vern and Donna Heinrich make a new seat cushion and a new canvas cover so it looked good, too. So that was how we spent the summer of 1989. We were to leave on Labor Day.

Everyone that went on the trip had to consign one head of cattle. They preferred they be Longhorn steers, but any kind of cattle would qualify. That made a good deal for us as many people that wanted to go did not own any cattle at all. I sold all the steers we had here right away and then started to sell some cows and heifers. When I had sold 20 head, I didn't want to sell any more so I turned down some sales. Of the nearly 3,000 cattle on the drive, I believe 75% were Longhorns. I don't know where they all came from but there they were.

Each wagon was required to have two designated outriders. They were to ride near the wagon and their responsibility was to assist the teamster in case there was a problem with the team. Kristin and Vern Heinrich were our two outriders. We had no problems but it was good to have someone ready to help if the need should come up. Kristin had planned to ride a young horse that she was breaking, but a couple days before the trip started the colt kicked her so she was pretty sore, but she toughed it out and made the trip but on an older horse. We had a horse we called "Bob" who was a good gentle horse, but not the best looking horse so we called him "Ugly Bob." Our neighbor Bob Anderson rode with us. He is at least 6'2", but his cousins called him little Bobbie. So we had Little Bobbie and Ugly Bob.

A great deal of advanced planning and organizing occurred before everyone was ready to travel. The cattle had to be branded with an M 89. Then they had to be trucked to the starting point at Roundup, Montana. Bob Kinney hauled the cattle as well as the wagons from the Glendive area. Most people hauled their own horses with horse trailers.

Four hundred wagons were too many to camp in one circle so the group was divided to make several circles for camping at night. Then in the morning each circle would follow single file until all the wagons and also the pleasure riders were on the trail. From the time the first wagon left camp until the last one left, it would stretch for 4 miles and take 2 hours. It was quite a sight to see. Our circle was often placed about in the middle of the line and we seldom could see either end of the line of travelers.

Many planning meetings were held prior to leaving. Don Walker was chosen wagon boss for our circle which was the green circle. (Each group was designated by a certain color.) Gene La Rowe was his assistant. Meals had to be planned for the whole week and food had to be packed. There would be no running to the store. Rose Marie organized each family group to furnish the food and cook a meal for the whole circle. We had breakfast early every day and supper when we made camp in the evening. For lunch we just had snacks.

Some 2000 people, mostly Montanans, made the trip but there were also people from all over the U.S. and also some from foreign countries. We met some wonderful people on the trail. Bob, our neighbor, had an uncle, Joe Gray, and his daughter Dot Georgi and her husband John from California who became our very good friends and still are.

When it was Georgis' turn to do the cooking, they did what is called the "Santa Maria Barbecue." It was big chunks of beef sirloin cooked on a barbecue grill with special seasoning and then sliced thin. It was the best tasting beef I had ever eaten. Everyone else said the same thing. They were generous enough to show us how it's done so now we serve it on special occasions and we always get compliments. Bob had served it prior to the cattle drive, but we had never tasted it before.

When all the cattle got gathered up to make the drive, there were 2800 head. That is a large herd. About 100 drovers kept them moving although with that many Longhorns in the bunch, it wasn't a problem keeping them moving. They just had to guide them in the right direction.

Each drover was required to bring an extra horse or two so there was a remuda to trail, too. Counting the teams, the pleasure horses, the wranglers' horses and the remuda, there were 5000 horses. Someone said they thought it was the biggest bunch of horses gathered in one herd since the Civil War. Then a Native American reminded them of Sitting Bull and General Custer. Anyway it was big and impressive. Pens were set up each night using portable panels. That was not quite authentic 19th century, but a rope corral and picket lines were also used.

We saw many different breeds of horses on this trip. Of those pulling wagons most of them were draft breeds or at least part draft, such as Belgian, Percheron, Shire, Clydesdale, and Suffolk Punch. The saddle horses were Quarter Horse, Paint, Appaloosa, Arabian, and various crosses. Some riders didn't have a horse of their own, but leased a horse from someone else. People with rental horses were able to do a good business.

It was a romantic time for one couple. They decided they wanted to get married on the trail. It just happened that Al Thompson, who was traveling with our green circle, was an ordained and practicing minister. He performed the ceremony one evening in the big Budweiser tent. A dance followed. Another couple and good friends of ours, Judd and Lillian Walker, celebrated their 50th wedding anniversary. This was also in the big tent. They are really spry and young for their age and rode all the way.

The Budweiser Beer Company was one of the corporate sponsors of the cattle drive. They brought two huge red and white striped tents. Each night they would have a tent set up at the camp site. They would have cold refreshments (beer and pop) for us when we got in. Everyone appreciated a cold drink after being on the hot dusty trail all day. While we were using one tent, there was a crew setting up the other one on the next camp site. Some days we could see the tent for miles before we got to it. It was something to look forward to each night. Sometimes there was music and dancing. The tent was closed at 11:00 each night and the camp would be quiet. Most people needed to get to bed because we had to get up early. It took a couple of hours to get breakfast, strike our tent and get the horses fed and ready to travel by 8:00.

While this trip was being planned, there were a lot of skeptics. They said with so many teams and all those riders, there were bound to be some terrible wrecks. Especially since nowadays there aren't a lot of real experienced teamsters. Also there are not a lot of well broke teams today. Having driven horses since I was a kid and having lived through some pretty bad wrecks and runaways myself, I expected there would be some who wouldn't make it to Billings.

There were quite a lot of old timers along and I suspect they helped the younger ones. I didn't hear of any major problems, but just a few minor ones. Several times along the way I overheard someone say, "Someone upstairs is watching out for us." Indeed I believe that was the case.

The skeptics also believed that there would be trouble driving that many cattle and getting them to Billings. The drovers were headed up by Jay Stoval and I believe they never lost a critter. There were 2 or 3 cattle got sore footed and had to be hauled in, but they had a full head count when they arrived in Billings. That was a very remarkable accomplishment by Jay and his crew.

When we arrived in Billings, the plan was that we would hit town shortly after sunup on Saturday morning. We would come in on Highway # 57 and turn left at the junction with old Highway #10. We would then proceed through the heights past Metra Park and then to the Billings Livestock yards. Despite serious objections from the authorities who tried to stop us at the outskirts of the city, the parade went perfectly.

An estimated 30,000 people lined the streets to watch us. There were people on top of buildings and even up in cherry pickers. The wagons come first with the outriders. Then the pleasure riders, the remuda came next and the cattle came last. We drove the teams at a good fast trot so we were sure not to slow the cattle down. If the cattle would not be able to go at their own pace, they may have tried to scatter some and the drovers would probably have had their hands full to keep them going down the right street. The same was true at the start when the herd went though Roundup. The cattle and loose horses were well trail broke by the time they got to Billings. The drovers did an excellent job as did the horse wranglers headed up by Lynne Taylor.

As we traveled from Roundup to Billing there was international attention in the news media. All the newspapers in the state gave it coverage every day

The wagon train in the Bull Mountains north of Billings.

as well as newspapers all over the world. There were helicopters from the television networks flying over everyday also.

This cattle drive was the biggest, most spectacular parade the city of Billings has ever seen. There were old timers lined up on the sidewalks watching with tears rolling down their cheeks, waving and cheering us on. It was quite emotional. It was a great privilege to be a part of such a wonderful event as the Great Montana Centennial Cattle Drive of 1989. As we were trotting down the street and people were cheering us on, I was thinking although I hadn't driven a team for many years, I would never be without a team again. It was good to have our nephew from Hawaii, Lowell Davidson with us on the drive. He rode one of our horses we called "Hooch" and was good help with

Rose Marie's nephew, Lowell "Dave" Davidson on Hooch.

harnessing the team. He understood teams from his boyhood in North Dakota.

The state of Wyoming had their centennial in 1990. They celebrated theirs with a wagon train. It was similar to the cattle drive in Montana except there were no cattle being driven and no remuda. If my poor memory serves me right, I believe there were about 80 wagons and a great many pleasure riders. We, of course, went along as did nearly the entire green circle. It was a fun trip, too. Lowell Davidson and his wife Betty came for this trip, too. We were glad to have them with us. We started at Story, WY. and ended at Big Horn, Wyoming. It was a 6 day 50 mile trip also.

Betty Davidson in Wyoming.

Chapter 30

Far And Away

One day in 1991 I was drinking coffee with the boys at the Trail Star Cafe in Glendive when Don Walker came with the news that there would be a movie filmed between Billings and Hardin. It would star Tom Cruise and Nicole Kidman and be directed by Ron Howard. It was to be about the Oklahoma land rush and they were calling for 400 teams and wagons with outriders and hundreds of extras for crowd scenes. It was a chance to get paid for what we had done the last 2 summers for the fun of it and at our own expense. Naturally we applied for a part in the show. Kristin (by then a C. P. A. and working for Peat Marwick in Billings) would again be my outrider riding Ugly Bob and Rose Marie got a job as an extra. There were quite a few people from the green circle who got jobs to make the land rush scene.

The movie was to be called "Far and Away" and it starts out with Tom and Nicole in Ireland where they fall in love. They have heard of free land in America and were determined to try for it. They managed to get to America, but had no money to get to Oklahoma where the free land was. Tom did everything he could to make enough money for him and Nicole to go west including bare knuckle prize fighting.

They finally got to the starting line where there would be a race to get the best location on the Indian land the government opened up for homesteaders.

That's where we came in. The scene we were in started with all the wagons lined up to wait for the signal to start the run. There were covered wagons, buggies, hayracks, stone boats and every kind of conveyance that could be pulled with horses. There were single horses to 4 horse teams. Also there were people on horseback and even some on foot.

The first day we got to the camp ground where everyone stayed while the filming took place. We furnished our own quarters. Some slept in tents, some in their wagons and some just rolled their bedroll on the ground. There wasn't much time for sleep anyway.

Breakfast was served in a huge tent beginning at 2:00 a.m. I wasn't the first one in line for breakfast. I usually managed to make it by 3:00 a.m. Breakfast was the only meal they served but they served everything you can think of for breakfast. They came around on the set with snacks throughout the day. Then at night we would cook our own supper. We usually got back to camp about 6:00 pm.

The second day which was the first full day we were there we got checked in and got on the payroll. After that we got a free haircut (a short one.) Some young guys didn't appreciate losing their long hair, but it was either that or go home so the hair went.

Then we went to the wardrobe shack and got fitted with period clothes. No one liked what we had to wear. I got heavy wool pants, a heavy wool shirt, wool vest and a wool coat. It was 90 degrees in the shade but we didn't have any shade. I got to wear my own boots and hat. Kristin objected to having to ride in a corset and long skirt but they said our way or not at all. She stayed.

We also had to go through a check with the wagons. We were told to bring things from home that would make it look like we were actually moving to a homestead. Then for safety measures they saw to it that we had the neck yoke tied to the wagon tongue and the wagon seat bolted down to the wagon box. They were very safety conscious about our rigs but what we had to do was pretty reckless.

The day before the filming started, the wrangler called us all together and explained that we were to line up at a starting line and wait for a canon shot to signal the start of the race for free land. The wrangler told us the main thing was he didn't want anyone hurt so we should drive our teams at whatever speed we thought was safe even if it was at a walk. He also said there would be a helicopter near by in case someone needed to get to a hospital in a hurry. Then he said we had to be ready to start for the filming area as soon as it was light enough to see. It was about a mile from camp to the stage area.

When we arrived where the scene was to be filmed, we all lined up in rows and waited and waited for the signal to start the race. We were to act like we were trying to be the first ones to get the best land. We had plenty time to visit during our wait. Everyone I talked to said they weren't going to run their teams as it was too dangerous. But when the shot was fired everyone whooped and hollered and urged their teams to run like they were afraid of being left behind. There were some accidents and the helicopter was put to use.

Everyone survived. Everyone had a thrill and some had a good scare. Several teams ran uncontrolled for nearly a mile until they came to a fence.

We made four runs a day for two days. Some teams became uncontrollable, like race horses before a race, and had to drop out on the 2nd day. They gave us the option of staying out of the runs if we didn't want to run again. We stayed in to the end. We didn't want to miss out on any of the fun.

When the movie was shown in Glendive, we were there, of course. We watched to see ourselves on the big screen. There were just a few people in our scene that was filmed close enough to recognize. We were not among them. So much for our movie careers, but we enjoyed it and we can always say we were in a movie with Tom Cruise and Nicole Kidman. And we got paid for four days. (Four long days.)

At the same time as the filming, a new book, "Photographing Montana, The Life and Work of Evelyn Cameron" was released by Random House. Rose Marie had arranged a book signing by the author Donna Lucy. Donna, her husband Henry Wiencek and their son Henry stayed with us here at the ranch and they became our good friends.

Chapter 31

Went To Europe

Rose Marie and I had been to Mexico several times and Canada several times, but we had never been off this continent together. Rose Marie had been to England to further her education one summer but I had never been to England or Europe. Being of Norwegian descent I should be interested in visiting Norway. I had a greater interest in seeing Spain. One night I was on the phone to my brother-in-law Steve (Finney) Farrington and during the conversation he mentioned that he and Jo Ann were planning a trip to Spain and Portugal. To that I replied, "Good for you. Spain is the only country in Europe I would really like to see." Of course he invited us to go along. It didn't take Rose Marie and me long to accept the invitation. Rose Marie had retired from teaching by then and I got Vern Heinrich to come and feed some cake to the cows and off we went.

We landed in Madrid where we saw the sights for a couple days before leaving for the south of Spain. Finney had the trip so well planned ahead of time that we were able to see most of the interesting and historic places. There is so much history connected to that part of the world that it was impossible to see everything in the two weeks we spent there. We saw a lot of old castles including the Alhambra where Queen Isabella agreed to finance Christopher Columbus on his voyage of discovery of America. Those old castles that are centuries old are still in remarkable condition.

We traveled by bus, train and taxi. The taxi drivers were interesting and usually quite helpful. If we asked if they spoke English, they would usually say, "a little bit." And that was about right. However, they seemed quite interested in listening when we talked among ourselves. Perhaps they could understand more English than they could speak.

There was quite a network of buses, complete with guides that would take tourists on day trips to interesting and historic places. We took a trip somewhere most every day.

We planned to spend a few days in Portugal so we began to ask people how would be the best way to get there. The reply from the Spanish people was, "I don't know. I don't think you can get there from here." There doesn't seem to be much cooperation between the two countries. In fact, we felt there was some hostility between the two countries. There didn't seem to be any public transportation that crosses the border, but we finally found a taxi driver that agreed to take us across. When we got across into Portugal, the driver became very nervous and hurried back to Spain. There was a train depot at the border where the taxi driver dropped us off. I forgot what city we were headed for but we got on board the train. When the conductor came to sell us tickets, the only money we had was Spanish money which made him very upset. We argued with him, trying to tell him that was all we had but he refused to accept Spanish money. I don't know what would have happened if a young fellow across the isle wouldn't have come to our rescue. He was an American living in Spain and working in Portugal and he exchanged enough Spanish money for Portuguese money to pay our fares. Luck.

It was fun traveling with JoAnn and Finney. They both have a great sense of humor and with Finney's personality, he can and does speak to any stranger he meets. The people over there are eager to talk to Americans, especially the younger folks who have had English in school. It gives them a chance to practice their English. We found the people very friendly and helpful.

We rode a train back to Madrid to board a plane back to the United States. Now we found the mood very different from when we arrived the first time. While we were over there the first attack on the World Trade Center had taken place and there were armed guards all over the place. Moving ahead a few years to 9-11 when the World Trade Center was completely destroyed, it just happened that Rose Marie was in France at the time. A lot of airline flights were canceled then but they got back OK. Kristin and I told Rose Marie, "No more trips to Europe."

Our nephew Lowell Davidson and his wife Betty from Hawaii had been to visit us a couple times and finally we decided to accept their invitation to visit them.

I don't care a lot for flying and Hawaii was a long way of not liking it, but it was worth it. Lowell and Betty have a beautiful place on the side of a mountain. They are in the construction business over there so it was no big task to carve a building site out of the mountain of lava. They both like horses and have built a stable and an arena.

While there we saw all the sights, including the largest cattle ranch in the world (The Parker Ranch). We saw Pearl Harbor, of course, and one night we saw a group of Hawaiian dancers. They were pretty, talented, and very limber and athletic. We enjoyed watching them.

We experienced a mild earth quake one night. It was a first for me. It wasn't strong enough to be mentioned in the papers but I noticed it. The people over there pay little attention to them.

Lowell and Betty own the biggest construction firm on the Island of Hawaii and we saw some of the fabulous hotels and condominiums they have built. Some were for famous and all for rich people.

We really had a good time the 2 weeks we were there and as this was during the winter, the weather suited us, too. When we went to the airport to return home, we were told the plane that we were to take had had some mechanical trouble and was late. That made everyone late to catch a connecting flight at Los Angeles. Most of the passengers were pretty grouchy and wanted to take it out on the ticket agent, like it was her fault. I waited until everyone else had been rescheduled and had time to complain before I went up to get our tickets. We had a couple hours to wait, so I wasn't in any hurry. This delay caused us a 9 hour wait in Denver, but so what. There wasn't anything we could do about it so why not make the best of it. Another day didn't make any difference to us. I was glad the mechanical problem didn't happen over the ocean with us aboard. When I got to the ticket agent, I was feeling sorry for her for all the verbal abuse she had taken so I tried to be a little pleasant. The agent told me, "Since you have been such a gentleman, I'm going to upgrade you to first class." Well, we were surprised but happy to accept. Going non-stop 14 hours makes one appreciate first class for sure.

Chapter 32

Prairie Fires

Farmers and ranchers are constantly on the watch for prairie fires. There are so many causes but probably the most common cause is lightning. I have come across more than one spot where a grass fire had started out in the hills but was put out by something. More than likely it started to rain so it didn't ever get too far. When a fire is sighted, the whole community shows up to fight it.

That is what happened two summers ago when a fire started along the Bloomfield highway. I don't know what started it, but the wind was blowing the smoke our way and it soon looked nearby. I didn't think we were in the direct path, but if the wind would have shifted just a little more to the west, the fire would have come down Lower Seven Mile Creek where we live. I hooked up a disc to my 2950 John Deere tractor and began making fire guards around the house and Bruce and Kristin's trailer house. I hollered to Bruce to get some water hoses hooked up, but he said the electricity was already out.

When I had done as much as I could around the house, I headed west toward the fire to see what I could do to help stop the fire. I drove the tractor about 6 miles before I got to the fire. It had gone several miles and burned up a lot of pasture but now had gotten into some rough breaks too steep for me. I put out a few smoldering cow pies and then started for home. The wind was still blowing strong when I got home about 10:00 p.m.

Our niece Katie and her husband Frank Castro and Rose Marie's sister Marian Maguire were visiting us and they helped prepare to evacuate but that didn't become necessary.

The next day an Air Force bomber and a couple helicopters came to dump water on it and eventually put it out.

There were over 100 men on the line and many stayed all night. The women of the community made sandwiches and delivered them throughout the night.

Some standing wheat was burned and several thousand acres of grass was lost, but no occupied buildings were burned and only one person was injured so it could have been worse.

My parents used to tell about a prairie fire that happened to them in the early days before the country was very well settled. It was started by a sheep herder who had started a fire to make some coffee and it got away from him. There were no fire trucks, of course, and very few people to fight the fire so it just kept going until it burned itself out. The folks were in a direct path of the fire, but luckily some cowboys came along and helped save the house. They lost their barn because a burning rabbit ran in the barn and set some hay on fire. There were some horses in the barn which they turned loose and tried to chase out but they refused to leave. They had to catch them again and lead them out. In panic situations like that a horse thinks the barn has always been a safe place, so he refuses to leave.

That fire didn't burn itself out until it reached the Missouri River in the Mobridge, South Dakota, area, about 250 miles away.

Chapter 33

Apache Joe, Reed Silvertip & Other Horses

Horses have always been a big part of my life. Maybe you can say I've been horse crazy. What I like about horses is what they have done for me. As I wrote earlier, when I was growing up in southwest North Dakota, we used horses for everything from moving cattle or sheep, branding calves or hauling hay. Then on Sunday we would think of something fun to do horseback.

I never claimed to be a bronc rider. I tried riding out of a chute, but it didn't take long for me to decide I was at the wrong end of the arena. If a horse bucked with me, it was all a matter of how hard. If a horse bucked me off out in the hills, I had no choice but to try him again. If a horse bucked me off near the corral, I just saddled a different one. I then had a horse to sell. I usually had gentle horses and they got used enough so they stayed gentle.

It's been 6 years since I've ridden a horse. I miss it a lot but since I have such poor balance after my illness in 1999, I don't get on a horse any more. At least I will never get bucked off again.

I've broke a few horses, but I don't call myself a trainer. I admire what a good horse trainer can do with a horse. When I was growing up, there were a lot of cowboys but not many really good horsemen. We had never heard of the Dorrance brothers or Ray Hunt or their methods of taming horses. So we got the horses in a corral and roped them (They were probably not even halter broke) and forced them to lead. After saddling them a few times and sacking them out, we would probably have someone snub the bronc to a gentle broke horse to ride them the first time. The idea was to keep them from bucking if we could. Or we might tie up a hind leg. They can't buck that way either and won't hurt themselves. In my case it was me that didn't want to get hurt. I've learned a lot from others over the years but I know there is much more to learn. When I was young I thought I knew quite a bit about horses but the older I get the more I realize I wasn't so smart after all.

When Rose Marie and I moved to Montana, we started raising Appaloosa horses. We also had a few quarter horses and later on some paints. This was after we had sold the Hildebrand place, moved to Bozeman for a year while Rose Marie got her masters degree at M.S.U. and came back to Glendive to buy the Mahoney ranch north of Glendive. When we moved to Bozeman we didn't have a horse that Rose Marie liked to ride so we went looking. Bill and Virginia Heavner from Manhatten, Montana, were Appaloosa breeders and they had a gelding that was well broke and gentle and would also drive on a single buggy. His registered name was Nugget Caprite, and we bought him. He was not a horse you would take to the horse shows but he had a really smooth gait and he was very good on his feet. He never once stumbled that I remember and anyone could ride him. If he didn't get rode for awhile that was alright too. He always stayed gentle.

Rose Marie was teaching at Dawson Community College then and I was working for Erickson-Nielson Agency selling real estate but we rode almost every night. Kristin was 4 that summer and needed a horse. We were able to borrow the perfect horse. She was about 13 hands and perfectly gentle. Cal Wyse owned her and I tried to buy her, but she wasn't for sale. Sweetheart as she was called had more kids to raise. So the next summer I bought Corky from Obert Kartevold. Kristin got along with him real well for a few years until she got Apache Joe, a registered Appaloosa.

Apache Joe was born here on the ranch. His dam was a Quarter Horse I had bought from the Kyd Cattle Co. at Three Forks, Montana. Her breeding was Scooter Bee and Band Play. Joe's Sire was Apache II, a great sire of Appaloosa show horses owned by Ward Fenton. When Joe was a baby colt and Kristin saw him, that's all she wanted to talk about. So for her Christmas present when she was 9, Rose Marie and I gave her Joe's registration papers all transferred in her name. When she opened the envelope and we saw the tears come, we knew we had done the right thing.

So the next thing was to get him broke. The next summer he was three years old and had never been ridden. Marvin Ley had been riding colts for us so he would be riding this one, too. Marvin told me if I would do some ground work and saddle him a couple times, it would save some time and he could start training him sooner. I did that with several horses I took to Marvin for training. I usually rode them a few times. Marvin was good with colts and in 45 days he had a good handle on Joe so we took him home. I rode him on the ranch that summer and then Kristin rode him in the arena. Letting a ten year old kid ride a three year old colt is asking for trouble and I know it, but those two got along so well I hardly worried at all. Kristin was getting to be a good little rider. She looked good on a horse. She had ridden in some shows on my old horse Black Nugget, who had been to so many shows he knew just what to do.

In the middle of October the NILE show is in Billings. In those days there were a lot of people showing Appaloosa horses and the Billings show was one of the biggest on our circuit. Kristin had been practicing with Joe and thought she was ready for the pleasure class for riders 14 years old and younger.

There was no school in the lower grades that week because of teachers' convention so off we go to the horse show. Kristin and I have Apache Joe and Black Nugget in the trailer and we are headed for some surprises. The teachers at the college weren't included in the convention so Rose Marie would join us for the weekend.

As we were driving down the interstate not many miles west of Glendive I happened to look in the rear view mirror and noticed a big flame in the pickup box. I had put a couple bales of hay in the box and they were on fire. We also had our suitcases and other things like my rope can and boot bag in the box. I stopped as quickly as I dared without throwing the horses off their feet. Kristin started throwing stuff out and I tried to pitch as much of the hay out as I could without burning my hands too bad. The first car to come along stopped and a man got out and gave a rare bit of information. He said, "Say, your outfit is going to burn up." He just stood and watched. Well, thanks a lot, mister. Kristin kept a cool head for a 10 year old whose favorite horse was in danger. Just when we were thinking we would have to unhook the trailer to save the horses, another car came along and stopped. It was a miracle. He was a fire extinguisher salesman with a car full of extinguishers on his way to give a demonstration at the Terry, Montana, schools. Right behind him were two oil field hands who jumped out of their pickup. They each grabbed an extinguisher, jumped in the back of my pickup, blew the fire out, jumped back in their pickup and sped away before I even had a chance to thank them. I had no idea who they were but God bless them wherever they are. How lucky can you get?

When I saw the hay on fire, I thought I would just throw it out, no matter what. But I can tell you it doesn't work that way. I did burn my hands some but it could have been worse. When we got to Billings that night I got some bag balm to put on them. We never did figure out what started the fire.

Next morning Kristin got her horse groomed and ready for the Western Pleasure Class, 14 and younger. It turned out to be a pretty big class of young kids with very little horse show experience. Instead of spreading out along the rail, the whole bunch rode in a close pack. Kristin got surrounded and ended up in the middle of the pack. Joe was getting irritated. He was not used to being in a crowd and being pushed around. He had his ears pinned back and he was grouchy. He waited until he was right in front of the judge and announcer and then he dropped his head and bucked Kristin off. She wasn't hurt, but I imagine a little embarrassed. Anyway she got right back on and finished the class. I don't believe Joe ever bucked before or since and he had to get used to crowds. And he did.

There weren't any shows close to home in the winter those days, so we had to wait until the first weekend in June when Forsyth, Montana, had a show. Kristin had been training Joe for the Western Pleasure. I had been cautioning her about pushing him too fast in the speed events like barrel racing and pole bending, because some horses get too hot and become hard to control. Her friends were there with older horses and were entering the speed events. So when she asked if she could enter the pole bending, I said she could. I noticed Kristin had some poles set up at home and had seen her walk through the pattern, but when she ran through them at Forsyth, I was amazed at how smooth Joe was changing leads. I don't remember if she placed for a ribbon or not that day, but it didn't matter to me. I was so pleased at the lead changes and how calm Joe was. The speed could come later and it did.

Kristin and Joe spent a lot of time together after that. They were good help when I needed it to move cattle and other ranch work. But Joe was in training for the shows. She entered him in all the youth classes and eventually the open classes. She even let me ride him in the team roping and other cattle classes.

We traveled to most of the major horse shows in Montana, North Dakota, South Dakota, Wyoming, and a couple in Canada. We hit the show circuit hard until Kristin went off to Carroll College in Helena. We were breeding horses then and going to shows was a way of promoting the horses. We were predominantly Appaloosa breeders, but we also had a few quarter horses and paints. We won our share of trophies, including a world champion trophy with Joe at the World Appaloosa Show in Oklahoma City. We are proud that Kristin trained a World Champion with a horse that we bred and raised here at our ranch.

Laura Brest, from Sidney was a very talented horse woman. She gave Kristin a lot of good advice about showing horses. Laura's daughter, Stacy, was the same age as Kristin and was a very talented rider so she and Kristin were competitors and also good friends. Laura was especially helpful in English riding which I knew very little about.

I went to a sale at the Kyd Cattle Co. at Three Forks, Montana, and bought 2 Hereford bulls and 2 quarter horse fillies. One filly was Joe's mother and the other one was a black filly of Silver King breeding. Rose Marie always wanted a black horse so I gave the filly to her for a graduation present when she got her masters degree. We called the filly Tippy and when she was old enough, she was bred to a Quarter Horse stud who was the last grandson of Joe Reed P3. That mating produced a bay horse colt. He showed a lot of quality right from the start and just kept getting better as he grew. We decided he was good enough to keep for a stallion. His name was Reed Silvertip. He was a yearling when we left the Bozeman area and moved back to Glendive and we left Reed with Bonnie Adkins to keep him and fit him for showing. Bonnie loves horses and horses love Bonnie. So she and Reed got along fine. When Reed got to be 2 years old I rode him a few times and then gave him to Marvin Ley to train. He turned out to be a nice horse to ride but we didn't use him much because he was usually out with some mares. After a couple crops of really nice colts, we sold him and some quarter horse mares to Vern Heinrich. That was probably a mistake, but we wanted to concentrate on raising Appaloosa horses.

Among the mares that Vern got was Queen Bee (Apache Joe's mother.) When I saw what a good horse Joe turned out to be I bought Queen Bee back. She was bred to Reed and had a super nice filly. When the filly was about a month old, Queen Bee got struck by lightning and killed. It was several days later I went to check on the mares and colts and found the filly lying with her head resting on its dead mother's belly. The filly was so weak from starvation, it could barely stand. I took it home and gave it some electrolytes with a tube and she got a little more strength so she could suck a nipple. Eventually she learned to drink milk from a bucket. I called her Little Orphan Annie. She grew up to be a very smart little saddle horse. She didn't get very big because of being deprived of her mother's milk, but she was really well balanced and liked to work cattle. If you held her back from working cattle the way she wanted to, she might buck a little. I started to team rope on her and she was becoming pretty good when I decided to breed her. She was in foal and running with some other mares in a 1/2 section pasture during the winter. She came up missing one day, killed by a mountain lion. We have had a total of 3 horses attacked by the big cats. The other two escaped but were torn up badly. We need better predator control.

Reed Silvertip sired many outstanding geldings. Some were out of our mares and some were out of Vern's. One Sunday we had a play day at Vern and Donna Heinrich's arena and 14 of the saddle horses were Reed's colts.

Branding yearling Longhorns. I'm on Annie.

I bought two Paint fillies from Harold Adkins before he and his wife Lucille went to Austrailia sometime in the early 1960s. They were both nice fillies. I sold one to Tom and Marian Crane. They and their daughters did well with her in shows. I kept the other one which I named Red Water Ree and bred her to a paint stud called Bill. He was an outstanding paint horse that I leased for a year from Bob Good of Custer, Montana.

The colt that was produced from the mating was a pretty paint horse colt. I gelded him and broke him to ride. He was as versatile a horse as I ever owned. I took him to quite a few shows and entered him in every class they offered including the halter class. He could do it all and do it well. We called him Red Water Willie.

When you are in the horse breeding business, you have to sell some. When it was Willie's turn to go, we took him to a sale in Rapid City, South Dakota. He sold to a South Dakota man who had two daughters who were interested in showing horses. A couple years later I met a cowboy who knew these people and he told me the girls had discovered other forms of entertainment and Willie was running in a pasture getting way too fat and not being ridden at all. What a waste. He was such a good horse and liked to work. I was wishing I

All these horses are sired by Reed Silvertip. The last horse on the right is Reed with Rose Marie.

had him back but as the old saying goes. I was "horse poor" and needed to keep them moving.

Now we sell horses on the Internet, or rather I should say Kristin sells horses on the Internet. The local market here is not good so she depends on the internet to advertise the horses world wide. She has been successful in selling horses to distant states like New York, Florida, Pennsylvania, California and most recently one went to Los Angeles to be put in quarantine before being flown to Australia.

Over the years I had several good rope horses. The first one was a Quarter Horse I called Buck. I was just starting to rodeo when I got him. He was a Texas bred horse going back to Old Sorrel and brought to North Dakota by Ernie Singletary and Punch Oglesvie. Evidently he had never seen much snow. The first time I saddled him after a snow storm, I wanted him to go through a snow drift. He started through all right, but then in the middle of the drift he became confused and just lay down. He soon got used to it.

After Buck died, I bought another good quarter horse named Square Butte. I got him from Leo Woodbury of Geyser, Montana. He was a good calf horse and team roping horse. Leo had trained him well. If he wasn't ridden pretty steady, he would get a little humpy but he never bucked hard and I could always stop him.

After Square Butte I used a couple of home grown geldings. Red Water Willie was a Paint and Flamingo's Twist was an Appaloosa. Twist wasn't the prettiest horse I ever rode, but was one of the best ranch horses I ever had. He had a little bigger foot than most quarter horses which I liked in rough country. He just never stumbled and he really liked working cows.

Then I used Apache Joe and Ugly Bob.

The last rope horse I rode was a horse I bought from Gene (Pete) Pedersen. I had him when I had to quit riding. I sold him to my nephew Gordon. I heard his wife Carla rode him quite a bit.

I wrote earlier about the mare Flossie that Dad gave me when I was 7 years old. When I got out of high school, I picked out another horse from Dad's herd. This one was a brown gelding but not a gift this time. I paid Dad $20 for him. He was 4 years old when I broke him. He was the first horse I ever broke. Dad thought he was part Morgan but mostly he was just a horse. He wasn't a big horse. He probably didn't weigh much over 900 lbs. But his endurance was outstanding. I rode him on some really long trips chasing horses and trailing cattle. He was another horse that would do anything I asked him to. I had never heard of Ray Hunt or his methods of gentling a horse. In those days there were lots of horses of all ages that were not ever halter broke. Horses were really cheap then because everyone was getting rid of their extra horses. Dad liked to buy and sell horses and he often would buy one here and one there, mostly from neighbors. If they were running loose and not halter broke, I would go after them with this little brown horse I called Jigs. If they were running with some gentle horses, I could usually crowd them in a fence corner or against a cut bank and rope them. I was tied hard and fast and the fight was on. I would let him fight the rope for a while before starting for home. I would chase him on the end of my rope in the general direction of home and when he tried to go back, I could stop him. By the time I got him home, he was fairly well halter broke. Times have changed. Now we use a goose neck stock trailer behind a 4-wheel drive truck.

Occasionally an old gentle horse would not lead very well. We had a remedy for that. It was a special kind of halter affair made with a lariat rope. It put pressure behind the ears and around the nose with enough leverage to be severe if not used properly. It was only for use on a broke horse that was stubborn. A couple tugs on the rope would surely bring them to attention and by releasing immediately there was no harm done. Using it on a green colt that was afraid and ignorant would probably create a head shy bronc. We called this gimmick the Ole Special because an old horseman, Ole Paska showed Wilmer how to use it and Wilmer showed me.

I never had the privilege of seeing Ray Hunt work with green colts but I am envious of his reputation. I guess I probably didn't get my horses as gentle as those who took more time with each horse. I didn't know any other way than to rope the horse, preferably in a small pen or round corral. It's not necessary to choke the horse down but with a rope on their neck you have a little control on which end of the horse is facing you. I learned the hard way that it's best to have a hold of the horse's head. I was petting a colt once without a halter or rope on him when all of a sudden he whirled and kicked me. He sure knocked the wind out of me. That was a lesson I learned at a young age. It might never happen again but a little caution here I think is prudent.

The mares we have here on the ranch are all gentle and can be caught out in the pasture. This is all because Bruce works with them and talks to them. I never know what to say to a horse. It is convenient to be able to catch a horse without having to corral them, especially nowadays because of having to catch them so often to give medications and vaccinations. Years ago we just let them run. We had never heard of West Nile and didn't worry about abortions and seldom even wormed the horses.

Nowadays horses are petted and groomed so they get gentle. It's handy to be able to catch a horse whenever you want to, but there are drawbacks to getting them too gentle. I don't like a horse that does not respect my space. If a band of mares are used to being petted, they are liable to become jealous of each other. If they have surrounded you, expecting to get some affection, one might push another one into you. If a horse is gentle enough to catch with a bucket of grain, that's good enough for me. But perhaps it's better to have them too gentle than too wild especially at my age.

Mother Nature used to raise our horses without any help from us humans. So there wasn't any need to handle them unless they were going to be broke to ride or drive. Some of the mares weren't even halter broke. Times have changed in the horse business, too, especially in the cost of raising them. I remember when Dad charged $5 to breed mares. Horses have certainly improved in the time since I was a kid as far as looks and conformation are concerned. I'm not so sure they are any more useful and I'm quite sure the old cold blood horses we used years ago were tougher. They had to be because they were used so much.

I believe horses should be out grazing whenever possible because they will be healthier. They will have fewer respiratory problems, less colic and other diseases and they will develop better feet, bone and legs. Unfortunately a lot of horses are raised where pasture is not available. Each operation is different and has to be run accordingly. Range raised horses do very well when left alone. When I was a kid there were lots of horses running on the range and sometimes we would see horses that didn't seem to belong to anyone, perhaps an old pensioner or one that got away from it's owner and drifted away. Horses were cheap those days. A broke saddle horse could be bought for $50 or less. The reason some people raised horses was because they didn't need to be fed and they would take care of themselves. So if there was any grass for them they were cheap to raise. If a hard winter followed a summer of drought it was hard on the range horse. There were no vet bills then because we had no veterinarians. That eventually changed but we hardly ever used one.

Sometimes mother nature will throw us a curve, but I have seen only about three winters when horses had a hard time surviving without being fed. With their ability to paw away the snow they do very well. Range horses do not as a rule seek shelter in brushy draws like cattle do. Instead they will back up to a small patch of brush out on a flat or they might go behind a cutbank. I think the reason for that is their one natural defense against predators, such as mountain lions is their ability to run fast and far. If they are in a brushy canyon out of the wind they become an easy target for a lion. So they like to be where they can see what is sneaking up on them. After a few generations of hand feeding and pampering they will loose that instinct.

Wild horses raised on man made or government sanctuaries do very well when left to survive on their own if they are not allowed to over populate their range.

Range horses and wildlife adapt very well to mother natures' time table, especially in eastern Montana and the surrounding area where the native grass is strong even in winter. In the summer when the grass is green the mare produces plenty milk for the colt. When the grass cures in the fall it's time to wean the colt and the mare gains weight for the winter. During the winter the mare looses a small amount of weight, which I think is good. The foal should arrive about the time the grass is getting green. It is best if the mare doesn't milk too much at first but increases as the grass gets better and the foal gets older.

As the grass gets better it is time to breed the mare for next year. If the mare is gaining weight she will cycle strong and will likely become pregnant on the first cycle. That is why I don't think it is a bad thing for a mare to loose a little weight during the winter.

In the early 1960s I bought a good black mare from Kenneth Slagsvold from Lindsey, Montana. She was bred to a good Appaloosa stud named Flamingo of AA. He was owned by Harold Adkins of Richey, Montana.

The next spring we got a fancy filly foal with a nice blanket. We called her Flamingo's Fancy and we planned to show her. So after she was weaned she got all the oats she wanted. Needless to say she got fat. I kept her fat and in show shape and she won her share of ribbons.

When she was six years old we decided to breed her but she didn't show any sign of cycling. I took her to Dr. Seekins in Belgrade, Montana, for an examination. The vet said one ovary had become inactive because of being too fat for too long but the other one would probably become active if the mare would loose 200 pounds. So I took her home and cut back on her feed and made her exercise and then took her to a stud and she became pregnant. She raised a colt every year for several years but I never again let her get too fat.

That is just one experience I have had with overweight mares. I think Mother Nature has this all figured out and we should pay attention. But love your horses and if you can't help feeding them a little too good it will probably be alright if they get enough exercise.

Ralph and Natalie Nelson and their four children have been our good friends for many years. Ralph was a good farrier and he shod our horses for years. When

Kristin was in school in Glendive she would go to their house after school if there was no one to pick her up. So Natalie was Kristin's second mother. Several years ago their youngest son Craig who makes his living shoeing horses in Florida came to spend the summer here in Glendive. I saw the opportunity to get some colts broke to ride so I invited him to stay with us. I like the way Craig handles horses. He seems to have patience but yet is firm.

One of the two year olds I wanted him to ride was a Quarter horse and quite wild-acting even though she had been handled some when she was a weanling. She was a nice looking filly and I thought she would make a good saddle horse for someone.

Craig did the usual ground work with the filly and in a couple days he got on her. Things went all right for a few minutes, but then she and Craig had a disagreement about which way they were going to go. So it was back to the round pen for some more basics and then Craig would get back on. Things would go smoothly again for a few minutes before a repeat performance of bucking. This went on for several days without any sign of improvement.

One day there was a team roping in Glendive. Craig is one of the really good headers around. I'm a heeler so that's another reason I asked him to stay with us for the summer. Craig didn't want to let the filly have a day off so he saddled her up and took her to the arena for a ride. The filly's pattern of behavior was consistent and perhaps even worse than the day before, but Craig didn't want to give up without making a little progress. When I saw that we were going to get a late start to the roping, I made us each a peanut butter sandwich to eat on the road. Craig takes his religion seriously, so it was natural for him to ask a blessing before eating his peanut butter sandwich. In his conversation with God, he mentioned he was thankful he could do the things he liked to do. After all the trouble he was having with the filly, I guess Craig must like a challenge. He was serious and I was amused and thankful Craig wasn't getting hurt. After several days with little or no progress, I told Craig we would quit the filly and I'd sell her to a rodeo contractor. So that's what I did and I never heard of her again. When Craig got to the house that day, he told Rose Marie it was a good day because he didn't have to ride the brown filly any more. The rest of the colts he rode that summer turned out well. One turned out so well I started to rope on her and planned to keep her, but she was the one killed by a mountain lion.

When Dad was in his prime and there were a lot of horses on the prairie, he would get called to come and castrate the stud colts. There were no veterinarians in the area, but Dad had a set of books that he studied and he had a reputation for being a self-taught horse doctor. He had no license of course and eventually a vet from Rapid City, South Dakota, advised him to keep his knife in his pocket.

He had been making a large circuit each spring that extended to a portion of northwestern South Dakota. After he got the warning, he didn't cover so much territory. This was before I was old enough to go with him to help.

Dad still got calls from around the neighborhood and after I got big enough, my job was usually to hog-tie the colts after they were thrown. They were put on the ground by catching their front feet and jerking them away from them. Then someone would grab the head and pull the nose up and back. That would keep the horse from getting back on its feet. Then I would tie the front feet together with a couple of half hitches.

With a loop run between the front legs I would catch the left hind foot and pull it up to the front feet and tie them all together. With another rope the right hind foot is pulled up toward the back bone and tied. This would expose the testicles for easy access. This procedure is for a right handed surgeon. The horse is lying with its left side down. If the surgeon happens to be left handed, the horse is laid on its right side and the hind feet are tied the opposite way.

Dad never actually taught me know to castrate horses but I had watched him so much that I felt confident I could do the job so when he died at age 84, I worked on my own horses and eventually some for friends and neighbors. Since I am now 81 years old, I will soon be leaving the job to younger hands.

I've been doing things with horses for at least 75 years now and I can say I've never been seriously hurt. I had a broken leg and a badly sprained arm. Both happened while I as on horseback, both happened while doing routine ranch work, and both were the result of being kicked by a horse. But I soon healed up.

I also played most every kind of sports from rodeos to checkers and except for a broken thumb playing touch football and a broken big toe playing softball in high school, I've managed to keep my bones mostly intact. But then I've seldom been reckless on purpose.

We tried to keep some gentle horses around for people to ride when they come to visit. One summer we had three teenaged guests from Sweden. They wanted to go for a horseback ride so Kristin saddled some horses and got ready to take them out for a ride. The one boy in the group had never ridden a horse so we gave him the gentlest horse. Robbie was also a bit lazy and when it was time to go he just stood still. Then the boy said, "O. K. horse vee go now."

Chapter 34

We Danced a Lot

The first 15 years of my life we lived in the extreme northeastern corner of Bowman County, North Dakota, which was in the extreme southwestern corner of North Dakota. Except for a creek that wandered back and forth across the ranch and a couple sharp rocky peaks, the country was pretty bleak. In fact it gave new meaning to "wide open spaces." There were some bushes along the creek but no big trees. There were some prairie dog towns and the usual other species of wildlife like rabbits, coyotes, badgers, and a few mink and lots of skunks, enough to make trapping profitable. Wildlife didn't have the cover to hide in so they were easier to see. One good thing we didn't have any rattlesnakes. Now that I've seen quite a bit of country I don't understand why Dad decided to pick such a desolate looking area to homestead when they could have settled in much better ranching country by riding the train 60 or so miles further west. However, now when I happen to return to look at the spot where our home used to be, I feel a certain nostalgia that I cannot explain. I would like to climb one of the peaks and view the countryside like we used to do as a kid. I still feel the people around Scranton, North Dakota, that I knew as a kid are special. But there are not many who are still living.

I feel the same fondness for the people I knew around Amidon and vicinity. The folks moved to the Amidon country when I was in high school and I lived there until I was 35 and got married.

Amidon was a great place to grow up, but we did have rattlesnakes. Lots of them. There was a good mixture of nationalities — a lot of Norwegians and Germans. There were Catholics and Lutherans and we all got along. There were a lot of kids my age. In the summer we played baseball and in the winter we played basketball. We went to dances all year long. I loved to dance and the faster the better. There were some very good dance partners at dances in Amidon, New England, Bowman, Rhame, Marmarth, Scranton and Gascoyne in North Dakota and Buffalo South Dakota. We often went to Scranton after the dance where "Fat" Perrington would cook a platter-sized steak for $1. Then we would drive the 40 miles home in time to get a couple hours sleep before we had to get up to start a new day's work.

There was a song that became popular in those days. One line I can remember went like this, "Those wedding bells are breaking up that old gang of mine." And that's the way it was. Bruce and Mary Lambourn were the first. They met in high school in Bowman and got married a year after they graduated. I felt honored to be the best man.

I was the last one of the bunch to get married and after Rose Marie and I spent one more summer being in show business, we left our home state of North Dakota and moved to Glendive, Montana, and we've been here ever since except for that one year we spent in the Gallatin Valley. I guess you can say we like it here. It's easy for me to feel sentimental about places I've lived and people I've known wherever I've been. I've never regretted the moves I've made but now I'm satisfied and think I'd like to stay here the rest of my days. We have a beautiful ranch, good neighbors, a wonderful daughter and son-in-law (they do the heavy work) close by so we think we are pretty lucky.

Chapter 35

Winters

I spend a lot of time in the garden in the summer. We enjoy fresh vegetables that we know are not raised with a lot of commercial fertilizer and pesticides. A garden tractor is a wonderful tool. It's a great improvement over the hoe. I did help a little with the haying but no bale lifting. Haying is so different from when I was a kid. We spent most of the summer haying and then usually ran out before spring. With a 5 foot mower and a team of horses and a pitch fork to load the hay, it went pretty slow. Eventually we got mechanized like everyone else.

Some winters were what we called open winters or mild winters without much snow. Then we didn't feed the cows hay, but we fed a good ration of protein pellets we called cake.

The winter of 1942 and '43 was the first winter I was home after graduating from high school. Wilmer was in the army and I was staying home to help the folks. The weather was mild and there was no snow until the last week of January. On the 25th it started to snow and it didn't quit until we had over two feet of the white stuff. There was no travel except with a team or horseback. The snow didn't drift all winter so it was at least two feet deep on the level. It was hard for coyotes to run in the deep snow so I was able to run some down with a saddle horse.

Elmer Morland had just finished high school too and was living with his folks, Jens and Selma Morland, who were close neighbors. Elmer had a girl friend living in New England, North Dakota, and he couldn't get over there to see her. Elmer thought of a plan. Sand Creek township owned a small road grader that was pulled with horses instead of a motor. It was light enough so four horses could pull it. Morlands kept a team in and so did we. Elmer called me to see if I would put our team on the grader along with theirs to make a four horse hitch. I drove the four horses and Elmer handled the controls to the blade and we opened the road to the highway. Elmer and Lorraine were married not long after that.

Eastern Montana and western North Dakota are sometimes called the banana belt of this part of the country. That doesn't mean we never get bad winters. One example is the winter of 1964 and '65. On December 14th, 1964 we had the mother of all blizzards. It snowed and blew with a wind chill of 75 below. We were living near Glendive but had a bunch of cattle and a little band of sheep on the Hillebrand place near Circle. I foolishly tried to go feed the stock. I didn't make it to the ranch but luckily I made it back home.

The winter of 1951 and '52 was a long and snowy winter in North Dakota. Wilmer and I were snowed in west of Amidon several times. The winter started in November and didn't break up 'til late in March.

1936 was a hard year for livestock on the range. The drought was severe and there was very little feed available. A lot of horses and cattle died before spring. That is as far back as I can remember as far as the weather is concerned. I believe we have more easy winters than bad ones in this area. Further east the winters are more severe.

Chapter 36

Dawson County Fair

The winters are all forgotten when it's time for the Dawson county fair. We just had our county fair at Glendive this past week. We started out with an open horse show on Wednesday. We have been involved in the management of it since 1961. Rose Marie does most of the announcing and the office work, but I don't help much any more. I did enter a couple of driving classes with my Haflingers on a nice buggy. I won the pleasure driving class and got second in the free style driving. Marvin Ley beat me in that one. Bruce showed a yearling stud colt of mine and got reserve champion. Bruce helps me so I don't have to lift the harness. That saves the old back.

After the horse show the Dawson 100 Club served a Santa Maria Barbecue for a fund raiser. I've been the president of the club since it began four years ago. The main purpose of the club is to raise money for improving the fair grounds and the Santa Maria Barbecue is our main fund raising activity. This year we served 412 people. We were pleased with the turnout.

The last day of the fair was the Ranch Rodeo. That's always fun to watch. The events are more like what cowboys do every day on the ranches. The contestants are local cowboys who come to town to play and to see who will be lucky that day. Teams of cowboys and one lady work as a team because the events all take several people.

Ranch rodeos are a relatively new sporting event. If there would have been ranch rodeos when I was in my younger years, I surely would have been a contestant. The team branding event brought back memories of branding calves back in North Dakota. I day dreamed of heeling calves and my wrestlers were Curt and Russ. We would have a lucky day and win the event. But it will never happen. Curt and Russ have passed away and I can't even ride, let alone rope.

When we get old, nobody wants us in the branding pen for fear we will get hurt. I want to say, "I didn't get this old by being reckless -- or dumb." But I keep quiet. I know it's just a fact of life and younger folks are thinking of our welfare.

1998 was the last year I was physically able to do things a 70 plus year old geezer should do. I had bought a nice 2 year old paint gelding at a horse sale two years earlier and was riding him quite a bit. One day neighbor Bob and I were looking for a bull that was missing. Bob was riding his big mule Sally and my little paint was having a hard time keeping up. (Sally is a fast walker.) It had rained the night before, making the trails pretty slippery and I was trying to be careful on the steep places. My little paint was getting irritated with me. When Bob and Sally went down a steep trail across a coulee, I wanted to hold up until they made it across but Paint had other ideas. He was so quick when he went to bucking down across the coulee, I lost a stirrup and very nearly fell off. I was not ashamed of the death grip I had on the saddle horn. By the time we went up the other side, it seemed to me we were going 100 miles an hour. When we caught up to Bob and Sally the Paint stopped and I was glad.

I had bought the horse to speculate on anyway and after this little episode I decided I'd let him go sooner rather than later. I decided I was too old to ride anything other than gentle horses although he never bucked again. I gave him to Marvin Ley to tune him up a little and improve his handling. We took him to a special gelding sale in Billings where he brought $4,000. He was a good looking horse, registered in the Paint Horse Association, and he made up for some horses that were not as good an investment.

Chapter 37

Branding At Amidon

Bob Anderson and I were running some cows together for a few years and one fall we were short some cows. They were Angus cows and running on some state land, which was so rough and rugged it would challenge a mountain goat. This pasture had no fence on the south side, because the coulees are so steep the cows didn't go there anyway. But they did and we had to go bring them back. They hadn't gone too far, but it was hard going to bring them back over a divide where they could get back to water and would probably stay. We started pushing these big black cows back trying to follow a deer trail which was a little narrow for these cattle and our horses, too. The cows would start up the trail and when it got really steep and narrow, they would stop. It would be difficult to get to the leaders to push them forward and to push, beat and holler at the back of the herd had little effect. It was only about 3/4 of a mile to the top of the divide, but it took us 3 hours to get there. I told Bob if we only had a couple Longhorn cows for leaders we wouldn't have had so much trouble. Longhorn cattle are easier to drive. They will move even if the trail is steep.

The last time I helped rope at a branding was in 1998 at my nephew Gordon's. He was running the old ranch Wilmer and I used to have in North Dakota. I was catching pretty well that day. I missed the first one though and I happened to see Bruce out of the corner of my eye and he was dragging one out by 2 feet so I thought I'd better bear down and get to catching. Things went better then. I just had to get that first miss out of the way. Gordon and Bruce changed off roping, too. There were 175 calves to brand and I think I roped nearly half of them. The next year at branding time, I had my broken back in a heavy plastic brace, I was not able to get on a horse and I couldn't swing a rope for sure.

Branding was an event I really enjoyed, but then I enjoyed most work we did on the ranch, as well as most all of my other endeavors throughout my life. I have always enjoyed working with my hands and if I could accomplish a little something each day, I was pretty content. I still like to accomplish a little something each day.

With the exception of the illness I had in 1999, most of the events I've written about have been positive. Perhaps it's because I like to remember things that way. I've always tried to think that everything will turn out alright. The truth is I don't remember much that didn't turn out well. I have indeed been lucky.

Going back so many years makes it hard to remember all the details but everything in this book is as I remember it. One event that keeps coming back to my memory happened to Curt Homelvig and me sixty years ago.

Curt and I spent a lot of time together when we were both single. We rode together for work and play and we traveled together to dances around the country. One night we went to Rhame to play basketball, (Amidon vs. Rhame.) That night Curt and I rode with Bud Mack from Amidon to Rhame with the understanding that as soon as the game was over we would go back to Bowman. Curt and I had promised two young ladies we would meet them in Bowman after the game. Bud was driving a pretty old car. It was a 1930 Packard. It had been a pretty fancy car in its day but its day had long ago become history. When we started out for Bowman after the game the lights wouldn't work on the Packard so Bud decided to stay in Rhame until daylight. So that left Curt and me on foot as far as getting to Bowman to keep our dates.

There was a wet snow coming down and a light breeze out of the northwest, but we decided to hitch-hike to Bowman. It was important that we get there. We no sooner got out on the road and stuck out our

Curt's high school graduation picture.

thumbs when a car came along and picked us up. But it turned out that the guy was only going four miles out which left us with twelve miles to go. We were confident someone would come by shortly and give us a ride. This was U.S. highway 12 and there was always traffic. Compared to today's highways this was just a little graveled trail. It has since been paved and also shortened. There was no doubt if someone had came along he would have given us a ride but no one came. We were pretty tired by the time we had walked the twelve miles. It was almost daylight and of course we were still on foot so we got a room at the Clara- Lincoln hotel and went to bed. We had stood up our dates, but we tried.

In those days most fellows wore dress pants instead of Levis so that night I was wearing gabardine trousers and with the wet snow coming down my left pant leg had gotten wet. By the time we got up the next morning the pants were dry but one leg had shrunk. So Curt took it to the dry cleaners and had it stretched. The girls eventually got over being mad at us.